The Yemeni cris

ꞁ

Kemal Yildirim

The Yemeni crisis - The Houthi insurgency in Yemen

Crisis Management and Conflict Resolution Strategies

LAP LAMBERT Academic Publishing

Imprint
Any brand names and product names mentioned in this book are subject to trademark, brand or patent protection and are trademarks or registered trademarks of their respective holders. The use of brand names, product names, common names, trade names, product descriptions etc. even without a particular marking in this work is in no way to be construed to mean that such names may be regarded as unrestricted in respect of trademark and brand protection legislation and could thus be used by anyone.

Cover image: www.ingimage.com

Publisher:
LAP LAMBERT Academic Publishing
is a trademark of
International Book Market Service Ltd., member of OmniScriptum Publishing Group
17 Meldrum Street, Beau Bassin 71504, Mauritius

Printed at: see last page
ISBN: 978-620-2-53066-8

The Yemeni crisis-The Houthi insurgency in Yemen

Table of Contents

The Houthis have other sources of support, however. They have reportedly
received funding from local supporters and sympathetic charities as well as from illegal
trade. Hussein Abdreddin al Houthi, a prominent Zaydi cleric and member of parliament
from 1993 to 1997, became a strong critic of President Ali Abudllah Saleh in the 1990s.
He accused the government of aligning too closely with the United States and Israel.
Tensions mounted further after President Saleh reportedly cut funding to Hussein al
Houthi in 2000. Frustrated by the Zaydis' poor political and economic status, he began
rallying supporters for anti-government demonstrations in the early 2000s. The
government issued a warrant for al Houthi's arrest, and his followers began clashing
violently with security forces. Al Houthi was killed by security forces in 2004. Since
then, his relatives and supporters have waged six uprisings against the government,
known as the Houthi wars. President Saleh accused Iran of supporting the rebellions.
The Houthis signed a ceasefire agreement with the government in 2010, but joined the
Arab Spring protests against Saleh one year later. Foreign Minister Javad
Zarif accused the United States of fabricating evidence related to the displayed missile

Introduction

What does Yemen mean?

Yemen is a country in Western Asia located on the southern end of the Arabian
Peninsula. It's bordered on two sides by water - the Red Sea and the Gulf of Aden -
and by Saudi Arabia to the north and Oman to the east.One etymology
derives **Yemen** from ymnt, meaning "South", and significantly plays on the notion of
the land to the right. Other sources claim that **Yemen** is related to yamn or yumn,
meaning "felicity" or "blessed", as much of the country is fertile. **Yemen** is a place of
religious importance and steeped in history. According to the **Bible**, Noah knew it as
"the land of milk and honey" and the Three Wise Men presented the infant Jesus with
myrrh and frankincense from its mountains. Some claim it is also the Queen of
Sheba's home The waves of protests, inspired by the Arab Spring uprisings in Tunisia
and Egypt, forced then-President Ali Abdallah Saleh to resign.

It is the poorest country in the Middle East. 41% of Yemenis are under the age of 15, compared to around 18% in the UK. The country spiraled into civil war in 2014 and, despite peace initiatives, fighting continues today. Today Yemen is experiencing the world's worst Cholera outbreak – 1 in every 51 Yemenis has been infected. Since the fighting started, 3 million people have been internally displaced. 60% of the population are food insecure and 76% of the population are in need of humanitarian aid.

The conflict has its roots in the failure of a political transition supposed to bring stability to Yemen following an Arab Spring uprising that forced its longtime authoritarian president, Ali Abdullah Saleh, to hand over power to his deputy, Abdrabbuh Mansour Hadi, in 2011.

As president, Mr Hadi struggled to deal with a variety of problems, including attacks by jihadists, a separatist movement in the south, the continuing loyalty of security personnel to Saleh, as well as corruption, unemployment and food insecurity.

The Houthi movement (known formally as Ansar Allah), which champions Yemen's Zaidi Shia Muslim minority and fought a series of rebellions against Saleh during the previous decade, took advantage of the new president's weakness by taking control of their northern heartland of Saada province and neighbouring areas.

Disillusioned with the transition, many ordinary Yemenis - including Sunnis - supported the Houthis, and in late 2014 and early 2015 the rebels gradually took over the capital Sanaa.
The Houthis and security forces loyal to Saleh - who was thought to have backed his erstwhile enemies in a bid to regain power - then attempted to take control of the entire country, forcing Mr Hadi to flee abroad in March 2015.

The conflict has its roots in the Arab Spring of 2011, when an uprising forced the country's long-time authoritarian president, Ali Abdullah Saleh, to hand over power to his deputy, Abdrabbuh Mansour Hadi.

The political transition was supposed to bring stability to Yemen, one of the Middle East's poorest nations, but President Hadi struggled to deal with various problems including militant attacks, corruption, food insecurity, and continuing loyalty of many military officers to Saleh.

Fighting began in 2014 when the Houthi Shia Muslim rebel movement took advantage of the new president's weakness and seized control of northern Saada province and neighbouring areas. The Houthis went on to take the capital Sanaa, forcing Mr Hadi into exile abroad.

The conflict escalated dramatically in March 2015, when Saudi Arabia and eight other mostly Sunni Arab states - backed by the US, UK, and France - began air strikes against the Houthis, with the declared aim of restoring Mr Hadi's government. The conflict has its roots in the failure of a political transition supposed to bring stability to Yemen following an Arab Spring uprising that forced its longtime authoritarian president, Ali Abdullah Saleh, to hand over power to his deputy, Abdrabbuh Mansour Hadi, in 2011.

As president, Mr Hadi struggled to deal with a variety of problems, including attacks by jihadists, a separatist movement in the south, the continuing loyalty of security personnel to Saleh, as well as corruption, unemployment and food insecurity. The Houthi movement (known formally as Ansar Allah), which champions Yemen's Zaidi Shia Muslim minority and fought a series of rebellions against Saleh during the previous decade, took advantage of the new president's weakness by taking control of their northern heartland of Saada province and neighbouring areas.
Disillusioned with the transition, many ordinary Yemenis - including Sunnis - supported the Houthis, and in late 2014 and early 2015 the rebels gradually took over the capital Sanaa. The Houthis and security forces loyal to Saleh - who was thought to have backed his erstwhile enemies in a bid to regain power - then attempted to take control of the entire country, forcing Mr Hadi to flee abroad in March 2015.

It began in the 1990s as a youth-orientated revivalist movement that wanted to defend the religious traditions of a branch of Shia Islam known as Zaidism.

By the 2000s, it was leading a stubborn military insurgency that enveloped tribal politics in the far northern governorate of Saada. Its objective was to defend itself and its allies against President Ali Abdullah Saleh's military.

When the Arab Spring began in 2011, Ansar Allah was a welcome supporter of the peaceful protests against Mr Saleh and actively participated in the National Dialogue that followed his fall. The group backed regional autonomy, respect for diversity, and the strengthening of a democratic state.

But as the interim government of President Abdrabbuh Mansour Hadi stalled in early 2014, Ansar Allah launched an aggressive military campaign in the north, defeating key military units allied to Gen Ali Mohsen al-Ahmar and the Islah political party.

This culminated in its descent upon the capital, Sanaa, in September 2014. Ansar Allah's stated aim was to install a more effective interim government to implement the outcomes of the National Dialogue. But clearly, it also sought military dominance in the north.

In the last year, an alliance with its former enemy, Mr Saleh, played a key role in transforming Ansar Allah into the dominant military and political force in the country.

For his part, the former president used the alliance with Ansar Allah to overthrow the Gulf-backed Hadi government and carve a more secure place for himself in future Yemeni politics.

Repression and Expansion

The source of Ansar Allah's power is principally domestic and political, not religious.

The Zaidi "Sada" - those claiming descent from the Prophet Muhammad's family, and who played a special role in the regimes of the Zaidi Imams that ruled North Yemen for almost 1,000 years until 1962 - were discriminated against by the leaders of the new republican Yemen because they were perceived as a threat. In the liberal period of the 1990s, some of the Sada emerged to search for a place for themselves in the republic. They formed two political parties, al-Haqq (Truth) and Ittihad al-Quwa al-Shaabiyya (Union of Popular Forces).

Al-Shabab al-Muminin (Believing Youth), the predecessor of Ansar Allah, was meanwhile founded by Hussein al-Houthi to revive Zaidi tradition in the face of effective proselytising among the young by Saudi-backed Wahhabis and local Salafists.

But it was the attack of the Saleh regime on al-Shabab al-Muminin that propelled the movement to the fore of Yemeni politics.

Hussein al-Houthi challenged President Saleh's legitimacy by claiming that he was weak and beholden to the United States and its "War on Terror".

In the context of the US-led invasion of Iraq, he chanted: "Death to America. Death to Israel. Curse the Jews. Long live Islam in the Grand Mosque of Sanaa." However, the target of the chant was Mr Saleh, not America or Israel. Mr Saleh attempted to repress the movement by force, but the tactics of the Yemeni military pursuing Hussein in the north alienated large sections of the population.

Ansar Allah's power grew from exploiting resentments against the Saleh regime, its military, and the leadership of the Hashid tribal confederation by the regime's key tribal supporters, the al-Ahmar family.

Ansar Allah knew northern Yemeni society and tribal organisation intimately, and those that fought for Ansar Allah against Saleh did not fight for Zaidi religious beliefs, but for freedom from oppression by an autocratic ruler.

Ansar Allah provided credible political and military leadership, not religious guidance.

The successful revolt of Ansar Allah in Saada was one of the key political failures of the Saleh rule.

A similar failure took shape in the south, where popular rejection of Saleh's regime was widespread, but without effective political leadership. Ansar Allah's support was drawn from those who rejected Mr Saleh's regime in the south, in the middle regions of Taizz, in the eastern desert of Marib and the Jawf, along with the educated youth activists of Sanaa. Ansar Allah joined the other anti-Saleh forces to forge the outlines of the liberal, post-Saleh regime.

However, the interim government of President Hadi - Mr Saleh's former deputy - floundered.

The National Dialogue took longer than expected, the question of the federal division of Yemen was not resolved consensually, and the rankling among political parties jockeying for position in the post-transition elections strangled the government while the economy deteriorated.

Ansar Allah began in early 2014 to take matters into its own hands.

It appeared to distrust the interim process and aimed initially to guarantee its military dominance of the north.

Ansar Allah had been the victim of Mr Saleh's military in the 2000s and the organisation, fearing the incompetence of the interim government, moved to guarantee its own security.

Mr Saleh played a key role in this last phase of Ansar Allah's expansion. In the interim period, the former president became an international pariah because of his interference in the transitional government.

In Ansar Allah, Mr Saleh saw a chance to change the balance of power in Yemen by defeating those that defected from him in the last days of his rule.

Ansar Allah attacked the Hashid tribal leadership of the al-Ahmar family, the Islah party, and the military units of the party's ally, Gen Ali Mohsen al-Ahmar (who is unrelated to the Hashid leaders). It defeated Mr Saleh's enemies in the interim government.

But Ansar Allah made big political mistakes. Its military wing moved fast to achieve maximum advantage without, it appears, consulting the movement's political strategists. Or else, perhaps, the organisation had no political strategy.

Ansar Allah retained the support of Yemen's political leaders and international backers of Yemen's transitional government as long as it adhered to the principles of the National Dialogue.

However, it broke those rules when it tried to dictate terms to President Hadi and he refused. Mr Hadi's resignation in January galvanised opposition to Ansar Allah in Sanaa and the southern and eastern regions of the country.

Now, Ansar Allah appears to lack a political strategy to unite Yemen's diverse political groups.

Mr Saleh may be hoping for Ansar Allah political mistakes to weaken the movement, leaving him in a key position to negotiate Yemen's political future.

However, Ansar Allah may have sufficient military advantage to consolidate its control of much of the rest of the country and repress any attempts by Mr Saleh to undermine the movement. Mr Saleh may be a prisoner of Ansar Allah.

Ansar Allah wants to consolidate its control of as much of the country as possible, particularly the oil-rich eastern portion of the country, and it wants to consolidate its political position, particularly with international recognition. While Ansar Allah may be able to further its military gains in the south, for example, where a very divided political leadership leaves the south vulnerable to manipulation, the Gulf states and the US appear intent upon denying Ansar Allah international recognition and supporting Mr Hadi's claim to leadership.

Yemen may see a long stand-off between Ansar Allah's north and President Hadi's south and east.

Why is there fighting in Yemen

Yemen: Areas of control and conflict

■ Conflict zones   ■ Yemeni government forces   ■ Houthi forces

■ UAE-backed anti-Houthi forces opposed to government

■ UAE-backed anti-Houthi forces not in conflict with the government

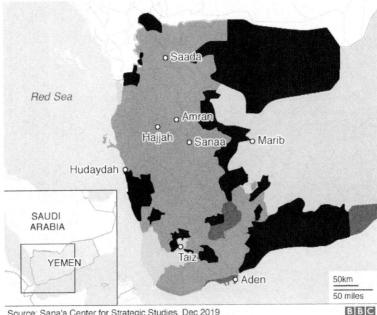

Source: Sana'a Center for Strategic Studies, Dec 2019

The conflict has been widely seen as an extension of the Iran–Saudi Arabia proxy conflict and as a means to combat Iranian influence in the region. In 2018, the United Nations warned that 13 million **Yemeni** civilians face starvation in what it says could become "the worst famine in the world in 100 years."

Why are the Saudis fighting in Yemen?

During the Houthis' southern offensive, **Saudi** Arabia began a military buildup on its border with **Yemen**. In response, a Houthi commander boasted that his troops would counterattack against any **Saudi** aggression and would not stop until they had taken Riyadh, the **Saudi** capital.

The **Saudi-led intervention in Yemen**, also called **the Arab coalition** (<u>Arabic</u>: التحالف العربي), is an intervention launched by <u>Saudi Arabia</u> in 2015, leading a coalition of nine countries from <u>West Asia</u> and <u>Africa</u>, in response to calls from the internationally recognized pro-Saudi[61] president of Yemen <u>Abdrabbuh Mansur Hadi</u> for military support after he was ousted by the Houthi movement due to economic and political grievances, and fled to Saudi Arabia.[1]

Code-named *Operation Decisive Storm* (Arabic: عملية عاصفة الحزم *Amaliyyat 'Āṣifat al-Ḥazm*), the intervention is said to be in compliance with Article 2(4) of the UN Charter by the international community;[2] but this has been contested by some academics.[3] The intervention initially consisted of a bombing campaign on Houthi rebels and later a naval blockade and the deployment of ground forces into Yemen. [66] The Saudi-led coalition has attacked the positions of the Houthi militia, and loyalists of the former President of Yemen, Ali Abdullah Saleh, allegedly supported by Iran (see Iran–Saudi Arabia proxy conflict).[4]

Fighter jets and ground forces from Egypt, Morocco, Jordan, Sudan, the United Arab Emirates, Kuwait, Qatar, Bahrain, and Academi (formerly Blackwater) took part in the operation. Djibouti, Eritrea, and Somalia made their airspace, territorial waters, and military bases available to the coalition.[5] The United States provided intelligence and logistical support, including aerial refueling and search-and-rescue for downed coalition pilots.[6] It also accelerated the sale of weapons to coalition states[7]and continued strikes against AQAP. The US and Britain have deployed their military personnel in the command and control centre responsible for Saudi-led air strikes on Yemen, having access to lists of targets.[8]

---

1 Yemeni leader Hadi leaves country as Saudi Arabia keeps up air strikes". *Reuters*. 26 March 2015

2 Nußberger, Benjamin (5 January 2017). "Military strikes in Yemen in 2015: intervention by invitation and self-defence in the course of Yemen's 'model transitional process'". *Journal on the Use of Force and International Law*. 4, 2017: 110–160. doi:10.1080/20531702.2017.1256565.

3 *"Is the Saudi war on Yemen legal?"*. IRIN. 3 April 2015.

Ferro, Luca; Ruys, Tom (2016). "Weathering the Storm: Legality and Legal Implications of the Saudi-Led Military Intervention in Yemen". *International & Comparative Law Quarterly*. **65** (1): 61–98. doi:10.1017/S0020589315000536.

4"Yemeni's Abed Rabbo Mansour Hadi arrives in Saudi capital". CBC News. 26 March 2015. Retrieved 26 March 2015.

5 "SOMALIA: Somalia finally pledges support to Saudi-led coalition in Yemen – Raxanreeb Online". RBC Radio. 7 April 2015. Archived from the original on 7 April 2015. Retrieved 7 April 2015.

6 Martinez, Luis (27 March 2015). "US Rescues 2 Saudi Pilots From Gulf of Aden". ABC News. Retrieved 7 April 2015.
Akbar Shahid Ahmed (10 August 2016). *"Obama Could End The Slaughter in Yemen Within Hours"*. HuffPost. Retrieved 8 October 2016.

7 *Rosen, James (7 April 2015). "U.S. stepping up weapons shipments to aid Saudi air campaign over Yemen"*. McClatchy DC. Retrieved 7 April 2015.

8 *Graham-Harrison, Emma (15 January 2016). "British and US military 'in command room' for Saudi strikes on Yemen"*. The Guardian. Archivedfrom the original on 16 January 2016.

The war has received widespread criticism and had a dramatic worsening effect on Yemen's humanitarian situation, that reached the level of a "humanitarian disaster"[9] or "humanitarian catastrophe",[10] and some have labelled it as a genocide[11]

In 2019, the conflict's status was described as a "military stalemate for years".[12]

Due to the global Covid-19 pandemic in 2020, Saudi Arabia needs to review its interests in Yemen. It now searches for an exit strategy and hopes that the Covid-19 pandemic makes it look like a humanitarian gesture instead of surrender.[13]

_____

Hawkins, Vickie (19 January 2016). _"Bombing hospitals and schools cannot become the new normal"_. _The Guardian_. _Archived_ from the original on 21 January 2016.

"House of Commons debate, Tuesday 12 January 2016". publications.parliament.uk (Daily Hansard – Debate, Column 681). 12 January 2016. _Archived_ from the original on 21 January 2016.

9 Borger, Julian (5 June 2015). "Saudi-led naval blockade leaves 20 m Yemenis facing humanitarian disaster". _The Guardian_. Retrieved 31 October2015.

10 _Durable ceasefire needed as 'humanitarian catastrophe' leaves millions suffering in Yemen – UN relief chief)"_. _UN News Centre_. 28 July 2015. _Archived_ from the original on 29 July 2015.

"European Commission steps up humanitarian aid for Yemen crisis". European Commission's Directorate-General for European Civil Protection and Humanitarian Aid Operations. 14 December 2015. _Archived_ from the original on 17 December 2015 – via _ReliefWeb_.; Original source: _"European Commission steps up humanitarian aid for Yemen crisis"_. 14 December 2015. _Archived_ from the original on 17 December 2015.

"Yemen crisis: How bad is the humanitarian situation?". BBC News. 24 August 2015. _Archived_ from the original on 28 September 2015.

11 _Ben Kentish (9 October 2016)._ _"Saudi-led coalition in Yemen accused of 'genocide' after airstrike on funeral hall kills 140; US says it will 'review' its support after latest attack"_. _The Independent_.

Bachman, Jeff (26 November 2018). _"US complicity in the Saudi-led genocide in Yemen spans Obama, Trump administrations"_. _The Conversation_. Retrieved 13 January 2020. As a scholar of genocide and human rights, I believe the destruction brought about by these attacks combined with the blockade amounts to genocide.

Taves, Harold (23 February 2019). _"Genocide in Yemen-Is the West Complicit?"_. Is there a genocide in Yemen? Based on the definition of genocide: The deliberate killing of a large group of people, especially those of a particular ethnic group or nation. The answer is an unequivocal YES.

12 "Yemeni Separatists Relinquish Control of Buildings in Aden". _The New York Times_. Reuters. 17 August 2019. Retrieved 4 September 2019.

13 "Saudi Arabia and the War in Yemen - Riyadh's Retreat". _Zenith Magazine_. 21 April 2020. Retrieved 22 April 2020.

Saudi-backed Abdrabbuh Mansur Hadi, running unopposed as the only candidate for president, won the 2012 Yemeni elections.[14] Since August 2014, the Houthis (or Ansar Allah), a Zaidi Shia movement and militant group thought to be backed by Iran, dissatisfied with Hadi government's decisions and the new constitution, arranged mass protests which culminated into their takeover of the Yemeni government in 2015, declaring victory of the revolution and drafting a new constitution when Hadi's provisional government had already expired its term. Saudi Arabia and other countries denounced this as an unconstitutional coup d'état.[15]

In military operations on the ground, the Houthis were supported by sections of the Yemeni armed forces loyal to former president Ali Abdullah Saleh, who was removed from power as part of the 2011 Arab Spring uprisings[16]Houthi leaders claimed[17]that Saudi Arabia was trying to break the alliance between the Houthis and Saleh's supporters, reports[18]claimed that Saleh's son Ahmed Ali Saleh had traveled to the Saudi capital to attempt to broker a deal to end the airstrikes. Saudi media claim that Saleh or his son had approached Riyadh seeking such a deal.[19]

By September 2014, Houthi fighters captured Sanaʿa, toppling Hadi's government. Soon after, a peace deal (known as the Peace and Partnership Agreement) was concluded between the Hadi government and the Houthis, but was not honored by either party. The deal was drafted with the intent of defining a power-sharing government. A conflict over a draft constitution resulted in the Houthis consolidating control over the Yemeni capital in January 2015. After resigning from his post alongside his prime minister and remaining under virtual house arrest for one month, Hadi fled to Aden in southern Yemen in February.[20] Upon arriving in Aden, Hadi withdrew his resignation, saying that the actions of the Houthis from September 2014

---

14 "Yemen President Hadi 'removes Republican Guard commander'". *BBC News*. 10 April 2013. Retrieved 12 April 2015.

15 Gulf Arab ministers condemn Houthi 'coup' in Yemen". *Reuters*. 21 January 2015. Retrieved 5 May 2015.

16 *al-Mujahed, Ali (31 March 2015). "Yemen's Houthi Rebels get boost from country's ousted dictator". The Washington Post.*

"Yemen leak: Collusion between Houthis and ex-president Saleh". Middle East Eye. 22 January 2015.

17 Yemen's Saleh proves to be a survivor". Al-Monitor. 29 March 2015.

18 "Yemen's Saleh proves to be a survivor". Al-Monitor. 29 March 2015.

19 "Saleh offered Saudi Arabia anti-Houthi coup for immunity". Al Arabiya English. 28 March 2015.

20 *"Yemen at War". International Crisis Group. 27 March 2015. Retrieved 6 April 2015.*

Heinze, Marie-Christine (30 January 2015). "The crisis in Yemen – The primacy of stability over real change". Qantara.de. Retrieved 12 April 2015.

had amounted to a "coup" against him.[21] By 25 March, forces answering to Sanaʿa were rapidly closing in on Aden, which Hadi had declared to be Yemen's temporary capital.[22]

During the Houthis' southern offensive, Saudi Arabia began a military buildup on its border with Yemen.[23] In response, a Houthi commander boasted that his troops would counterattack against any Saudi aggression and would not stop until they had taken Riyadh, the Saudi capital.[24]

On 25 March, Hadi called on the UN Security Council to authorise "willing countries that wish to help Yemen to provide immediate support for the legitimate authority by all means and measures to protect Yemen and deter the Houthi aggression".[25]

Yemen's foreign minister, Riad Yassin, requested military assistance from the Arab League on 25 March, amid reports that Hadi had fled his provisional capital.[26] On 26 March, Saudi state TV station Al-Ekhbariya TV reported that Hadi arrived at a Riyadh airbase and was met by Saudi Defense Minister Mohammad bin Salman Al Saud. His route from Aden to Riyadh was not immediately known.[27]

At a summit of the Arab League held in Sharm El-Sheikh, Egypt, on 28–29 March, President Hadi again repeated his calls for international intervention in the fighting. A number of League members pledged their support to Hadi's government during that meeting.[28]

----

21 "Yemen's Hadi withdraws resignation, as UN pushes for dialogue". Middle East Eye. 24 February 2015.

"Yemen's ousted president withdraws resignation". Al Jazeera. 24 February 2015.

22 "Al Subaihi captured and Lahj falls as Houthis move on Aden". Yemen Times. 25 March 2015. Retrieved 26 March 2015.

23 "Exclusive: Saudi Arabia building up military near Yemen border – U.S. officials". Reuters. 24 March 2015. Retrieved 25 March 2015.

24 Almasmari, Hakim (24 March 2015). "Yemen's Houthi Militants Extend Push Southward". The Wall Street Journal. Retrieved 25 March 2015.

25 Yemen's President Hadi asks UN to back intervention". BBC News. 25 March 2015.

26 Beck, John (25 March 2015). "Saudi Arabia Launches Airstrikes in Yemen as President Flees Amid Rebel Advance". Vice News. Retrieved 25 March2015.

(in Vietnamese) "Phiến quân Shiite tấn công, tổng thống Yemen bỏ chay"Archived 2 April 2015 at the Wayback Machine. 25 March 2015. Retrieved 26 March 2015

27 "Yemeni's Abed Rabbo Mansour Hadi arrives in Saudi capital". CBC News. 26 March 2015. Retrieved 26 March 2015.

28 "Arab League summit wraps up with plan for pan-Arab force". Deutsche Welle. 29 March 2015.

"Yemen crisis tops agenda as Arab League summit opens". Deutsche Welle. 28 March 2015.

Many ancient cultural heritage sites in Yemen have been destroyed and damaged by Saudi-led coalition airstrikes including some as old as 3,000 years.[29]

According to the Saudi news outlet Al Arabiya, Saudi Arabia contributed 100 warplanes and 150,000 soldiers to the military operation. Reuters indicated that planes from Egypt, Morocco, Jordan, Sudan, Kuwait, the United Arab Emirates, Qatar and Bahrain were taking part.[30] Egypt had previously sent four warships supporting the Saudi naval blockade.[31]

The UAE contributed 30 fighter jets, Kuwait sent 15 (understood to be three squadrons of F/A-18 Hornet aircraft),[32] Bahrain sent 15, Qatar 10, Jordan and Morocco six each and Sudan four.[33]

The operation was declared over on 21 April 2015.[34]

Air campaign - March 2015

In March 2015 in a joint statement, the member-states of the Gulf Cooperation Council (with the exception of Oman) said they had decided to intervene against the Houthis at the request of Hadi's government.[35]

The coalition declared Yemeni airspace to be a restricted area, with King Salman declaring the RSAF to be in full control of the zone.[36] Saudi Arabia began airstrikes, reportedly relying on US intelligence reports and surveillance images to select and hit targets, including weapons, aircraft[36]on the ground and air defences.[110] Al Jazeera reported that Mohammed Ali al-Houthi, a Houthi commander appointed in

---

29 Taylor, Adam (5 June 2015). "The world may be ignoring the destruction of cultural treasures in Yemen". *The Washington Post*. Retrieved 9 February2018.

30 *"Factbox: Saudi-led coalition against Yemen's Houthis". Reuters. 10 April 2015.*

Steve Almasy; Jason Hanna (25 March 2015). "Saudi Arabia launches airstrikes in Yemen". CNN.

31 "Who is arming the Yemen war? (And is anyone planning to stop?) | Reinventing Peace". 28 February 2018. Retrieved 16 February 2019.

32 Saudi and Arab allies bomb Houthi positions in Yemen". 26 March 2015. Retrieved 26 March 2014.

33 *"Sudan denies plane shot down by Yemen's Houthis". World Bulletin. 28 March 2015. Retrieved 28 March 2015.*

Gulf states consider Yemen ground offensive to halt Houthi rebel advance". The Guardian. 26 March 2015. Retrieved 26 March 2014.

34 "Yemen conflict: Saudi Arabia ends air campaign". *BBC News*. 21 April 2015. Retrieved 21 April 2015

35 "Saudi and Arab allies bomb Houthi positions in Yemen". Al Jazeera. 26 March 2015. Retrieved 25 March 2015

36 Saudi Arabia launches airstrikes in Yemen". CNN. 26 March 2015. Retrieved 25 March 2015.

February as president of the Revolutionary Committee, was injured and three other Houthi commanders were killed by airstrikes in Sana'a.[37]

Strikes on 26 March also hit Al Anad Air Base, a former US special operations forces facility in Lahij Governorate seized by Houthis earlier in the week.[112] The targets reportedly included the Houthi-controlled missile base in Sana'a and its fuel depot. [2] Strikes overnight also targeted Houthis in Taiz and Sa'dah. Thousands demonstrated in Sana'a against the intervention, which ex-president Ali Abdullah Saleh also condemned. In Taiz thousands came out supporting Hadi and Saudi Arabia.[38]

The scope of strikes expanded further on 27 March, with a radar installation in the Ma'rib Governorate and an airbase in the Abyan Governorate coming under air attack. The commander of the operation dismissed reports of civilian casualties, saying airstrikes were being carried out with precision.[39] Additional strikes early on the next day hit targets in Al Hudaydah, Sa'dah and the Sana'a area, as well as Ali Abdullah Saleh's main base. Rumours indicated Saleh fled to Sanhan, on the outskirts of the Houthi-controlled capital. [115] An Aden government official said Saudi strikes destroyed a long-range missile facility controlled by the Houthis.[40]

The Houthis claimed to have shot down a Sudanese Air Force plane over northern Sana'a and captured its pilot on 28 March. The Sudanese government denied that any of its four warplanes had come under fire or been shot down.[41] On the previous day, the Houthis claimed to have shot down a "hostile" Saudi drone in Sana'a.[42]

Airstrikes hit an arms depot, military airbase and special forces headquarters in Sana'a early on 29 March. A weapons depot outside Sana'a was destroyed, causing damage to an airport and planes on the ground. Sa'dah and Al Hudaydah were targeted as well. Brigadier General Ahmed Asiri, the coalition's spokesman, said Saudi artillery and Apache attack helicopters were mobilised to "deter" Houthi fighters massing on the border with Saudi Arabia.[43]

On 30 March, at least 40 people including children were killed and 200 were injured[119] by an airstrike that hit Al-Mazraq refugee camp near a military installation in northern district

---

37 "Saudis launch air campaign to defend Yemen government". Al Jazeera. 25 March 2015. Retrieved 1 April 2015.

38 "Coalition jets continue to hit Houthi targets in Yemen". Al Jazeera. 27 March 2015. Retrieved 26 March 2015.

39 Yeranian, Edward (27 March 2015). "Egyptian, Saudi Vessels Approach Yemen Coast". Voice of America. Retrieved 27 March 2015.

40 Saudi operation hit Yemen base holding long-range missiles". World Bulletin. 28 March 2015. Retrieved 28 March 2015.

41 "Sudan denies plane shot down by Yemen's Houthis"

42 Yemen's Houthis shoot down drone in Sanaa: TV". www.aa.com.tr.

43 "Fresh Saudi-led strikes hit Houthi targets in Yemen". Al Jazeera. 29 March 2015. Retrieved 28 March 2015.

of Haradh, international organizations said. Airstrikes also hit areas near the presidential palace in Sana'a,[44] as well as Aden International Airport.[45]

Food storage of Yemen Economic Corporation in Hodeidah was destroyed by three coalition strikes on 31 March.[46] Airstrikes were not limited to the Yemeni mainland. Missiles struck homes on the island of Perim, according to residents who fled by boat to Djibouti.[47]

April 2015

Dozens of casualties came from an explosion at a dairy and oil factory in Al Hudaydah, which was variously blamed on an airstrike or a rocket from a nearby military base on 1 April. Medical sources reported 25 deaths, while the Yemen Army said 37 were killed and 80 wounded.[48] Airstrikes also hit targets in Sa'dah on 1 April.[49]

Despite persistent airstrikes, Houthi and allied units continued to advance on central Aden, backed by tanks and heavy artillery.[50] Houthis seized the presidential palace on 2 April, but reportedly withdrew after overnight air raids early the next day.[51] Coalition planes also airdropped weapons and medical aid to pro-Hadi fighters in Aden.[52]

The International Committee of the Red Cross announced on 5 April that it had received permission from the coalition to fly medical supplies and aid workers into Sana'a and was awaiting permission to send a surgical team by boat to Aden. The coalition said it had set up a special body to coordinate aid deliveries to Yemen.[53]

---

44 Al-Haj, Ahmed (30 March 2015). "Yemeni Rebels Shell Aden as Saudi Launches More Airstrikes". ABC News. Retrieved 30 March 2015.

45 "Dozens killed as Yemen's Houthis shell Aden, Saudi jets bomb airport". The Sydney Morning Herald. 31 March 2015. Retrieved 31 March 2015.

46 Yemeni civilians struggle to get by amid conflict". 6 April 2015. Retrieved 8 April 2015.

47 Elbagir, Nima (9 April 2015). "'A window into hell:' Desperate Yemenis flee Saudi airstrikes by boat". CNN. Retrieved 9 April 2015.

48 "Explosion at Yemen factory kills at least 25: residents, medics". Reuters. 1 April 2015. Retrieved 1 April 2015.

49 Hatem, Mohammed (31 March 2015). "Saudi Coalition Hits Houthi Stronghold as Aden Battle Rages". Bloomberg News. Retrieved 1 April 2015.

50 al-Mujahed, Ali (1 April 2015). "Rebel forces push farther into key Yemeni port city of Aden". The Washington Post.

  1. ^ "Yemen Houthi fighters backed by tanks reach central Aden". Reuters. 1 April 2015.

51 "Yemen rebels quit Aden palace after air raids: Senior official". Zee News. 3 April 2015. Retrieved 2 April 2015.

52 "Saudis airdrop arms to Aden defenders, Houthis pull back". Hindustan Times. 3 April 2015. Retrieved 3 April 2015.

53 Red Cross given permission to deliver aid to Yemen". Al Jazeera. 6 April 2015. Retrieved 5 April 2015.

On 6 April, airstrikes began before sunset and struck targets in western Sana'a, Sa'dah and the Ad Dali' Governorate, a supply route for Houthis in the Battle of Aden[54]

Airstrikes on 7 April hit a Republican Guard base in the Ibb Governorate, injuring 25 troops. Yemeni sources claimed three children at a nearby school were killed by the attack,[55] while six were injured.[56]

The Parliament of Pakistan voted against military action on 10 April, despite a request from Saudi Arabia that it join the coalition.[57]

Airstrikes launched on 12 April, against the base of the 22nd Brigade of the Yemeni Republican Guard in the Taiz Governorate struck both the brigade and a nearby village inhabited by members of the Al-Akhdam minority community, killing eight civilians and injuring more than ten others.[58] On 17 April, both the GCC coalition's spokesman called by Saudi broadcaster Al-Ehkbariya TV and a commander of the pro-Hadi rebels on the ground said airstrikes had intensified, focusing on both Sana'a and Taiz.[59] One strike on the Republican Palace in Taiz killed 19 pro-Houthi gunmen.

Naval role

Egypt and Saudi Arabia committed warships to support coalition operations.[139] Somalia offered its airspace and territorial waters.[60] Four Egyptian Navy vessels steamed toward the Gulf of Aden after operations began.[61] Riyadh requested access to Somali airspace and waters to carry out operations.[62] On 27 March, the Egyptian military said a squadron

---

54 "Fierce fighting as rebels move on holdouts in Yemen's Aden". *Houston Chronicle*. 6 April 2015. Retrieved 6 April 2015.
"Securing key Yemen strait a priority for Egypt, says Sisi". *Times of Oman*. 4 April 2015. Retrieved 7 April 2015.
"Yemen says Saudi airstrikes hit school, injuring students". CNN. 7 April 2015. Retrieved 7 April 2015.

55 *"Saudi-led airstrikes hit Yemen's south amid ground fighting". Boston Herald. 7 April 2015. Retrieved 7 April 2015.*

56 *Mukhashaf, Mohammed (10 April 2015). "Pakistan declines Saudi call for armed support in Yemen fight". Reuters. Retrieved 10 April 2015.*

57 *Mukhashaf, Mohammed (10 April 2015). "Pakistan declines Saudi call for armed support in Yemen fight". Reuters. Retrieved 10 April 2015.*

58 Civilians Killed by a Coalition Strike on a Republican Guards Brigade in Taiz". *Yemen Times*. 12 April 2015. Retrieved 12 April 2015.

59 "Al-Qaida in Yemen Takes Massive Weapons Depot From Army". ABC News. Associated Press. 17 April 2015.

60 "SOMALIA: Somalia finally pledges support to Saudi-led coalition in Yemen – Raxanreeb Online". RBC Radio. 7 April 2015. Archived from the original on 7 April 2015. Retrieved 7 April 2015.

61 Saudi Arabia leads airstrikes against Yemen's Houthi rebels". Al Jazeera America. 26 March 2015. Retrieved 26 March 2015

62 "Saudi led coalition request Somalia to use its airspace to attack Houthi rebels". *Somali Current*. 26 March 2015. Archived from the original on 9 July 2015. Retrieved 6 October 2019.

of Egyptian and Saudi warships took up positions at the Bab al-Mandab strait.[63] The Saudi military threatened to destroy any ship attempting to make port.[64]

The Royal Saudi Navy evacuated diplomats and United Nations staff from Aden to Jeddah on 28 March.[65]

Witnesses told Reuters that Egyptian warships bombarded Houthi positions as they attempted to advance on Aden on 30 March.[66] Warships again fired on Houthi positions at Aden International Airport on or about 1 April.[67]

Djibouti foreign minister Mahmoud Ali Youssouf said the Houthis placed heavy weapons and fast attack boats on Perim and a smaller island in the Bab al-Mandab strait. He warned that "the prospect of a war in the strait of Bab al-Mandab is a real one" and said the weapons posed "a big danger" to his country, commercial shipping traffic, and military vessels. He called on the coalition to clear the islands, which he said included missiles and long-range cannons.[68]

On 4 April, Egyptian President Abdel Fattah el-Sisi called protecting Red Sea shipping and securing the Bab al-Mandab "a top priority for Egypt's national security".[69]

On 15 April, coalition spokesman Saudi Brigadier General Ahmed Al-Asiri, said that its warships were focusing on protecting shipping routes and screening ships heading to port for shipments intended for the Houthis.[70]

The US Navy provided support to the naval blockade, halting and searching vessels suspected of carrying Iranian arms to the Houthis.[71] On 21 April, the United States announced it was deploying warships to Yemeni waters to monitor Iranian ships.[148] The US in particular noted a convoy of Iranian vessels, which US authorities said could potentially be carrying weapons to Houthi fighters in contravention of UN sanctions. [149] The US reported that the Iranian convoy reversed course on 23 April.[150]

----

63 Yeranian, Edward (27 March 2015). "Egyptian, Saudi Vessels Approach Yemen Coast". Voice of America. Retrieved 27 March 2015.

64 "Saudi-led coalition strikes rebels in Yemen, inflaming tensions in region". CNN. 26 March 2015. Retrieved 26 March 2015.

65 "Diplomats and U.N. staff flee Yemen as Houthis target Aden". Reuters. 28 March 2015. Retrieved 28 March 2015.

66 "Warships shell Houthis outside Yemeni city of Aden -witnesses". Thomson Reuters Foundation. 30 March 2015. Retrieved 30 March 2015.

67 Hatem, Mohammed (31 March 2015). "Saudi Coalition Hits Houthi Stronghold as Aden Battle Rages". Bloomberg News. Retrieved 1 April 2015.

68 Richardson, Paul (2 April 2015). "Yemeni Rebels Strengthen Positions at Entrance to Red Sea". Bloomberg News. Retrieved 2 April 2015.

69 "Securing key Yemen strait a priority for Egypt, says Sisi". Times of Oman. 4 April 2015. Retrieved 7 April 2015.

70 "Day 21 April 15, 2015: Saudi Ministry of Defense Briefing". Saudi Ministry of Defense. 15 April 2015.

71 Abi-Habib, Maria; Entous, Adam (12 April 2015). "U.S. Widens Role in Saudi-led Campaign Against Houthi Rebels in Yemen". The Wall Street Journal. Retrieved 13 April 2015.

Ground clashes

Sudan said it was stationing ground troops in Saudi Arabia.[151] The Special Forces of the Bahrain Defence Force, Taskforce 11, were also deployed to Yemen.[152]

Between 31 March and April, Saudi and Houthi forces reportedly traded artillery and rocket fire across the border between SA and Yemen.[121][153] A Saudi border guard was killed on 2 April, the campaign's first confirmed coalition casualty.[154] Followed by another two soldiers killed the next day.[155] An Egyptian truck driver was killed by Houthi shelling.[156]

SA reportedly began removing sections of the Saudi–Yemen barrier fence along its border with the Sa'dah and Hajjah governorates on 3 April. The purpose of the removal was not immediately clear.[157]

On 12 April, members of the Takhya tribe launched an attack on a Saudi base after several of its members died in an airstrike. Weapons and ammunition were taken.[158][159][160]

On 19 April, as Houthi leader Abdul-Malek El-Houthi accused SA of planning to invade Yemen,[161] Asiri claimed that coalition forces had information regarding a planned Houthi incursion into SA.[162] A Saudi border guard died on 19 April and two others were injured from gunfire and mortar shelling across the border.[163]

On 21 April, the Saudi Defence Ministry declared it was ending the campaign of airstrikes because it had "successfully eliminated the threat" to its security posed by Houthi ballistic and heavy weaponry.[164] It announced the start of a new phase codenamed Operation Restoring Hope.[165] In a televised address, Hadi said the end of airstrikes had come at his request and thanked the Arab coalition for their support.[166]

Earlier that day King Salman ordered the Saudi National Guard to join the military operation.[167] Air and naval strikes continued despite the announcement that *Decisive Storm* had ended.

Both the Omani[72] and Iranian[73] governments said they welcomed the end of airstrikes. On 22 April, Oman presented a seven-point peace deal to both parties. The proposed peace treaty entailed the reinstatement of Hadi's government and the evacuation of Houthi fighters from major cities.[74]

On 8 May, Saudi Arabia announced a five-day ceasefire set to start on 12 May,[75] following heavy pressure from the US.[76] Later in the day, Saudi airplanes dropped leaflets in the Saada Governorate warning of airstrikes throughout the area.[77] Houthi

---

72 "Yemen rivals battle on despite declared end to Saudi raids". *Reuters*. 22 April 2015. Retrieved 22 April 2015.

73 "Saudi Arabia declares end to Yemen air strikes after four weeks of bombing". *The Guardian*. 22 April 2015.

74 "Yemen rivals battle on despite declared end to Saudi raids". *Reuters*. 22 April 2015. Retrieved 22 April 2015.

75 Rubin, Alissa J.; Fahim, Kareem (8 May 2015). *"Saudi Arabia Announces Cease-Fire in Yemen". The New York Times*.

76 "The war in Yemen: From Aden to Camp David". *The Economist*. 14 May 2015. Retrieved 18 May 2015.

77 Arab coalition warns Yemenis to leave Saada province". *Al Jazeera*. 9 May 2015. Retrieved 6 April 2020.

spokesman Mohamed al-Bukhaiti later told the BBC that the ceasefire had not been formally proposed and the Houthis would not respond until a plan was properly laid out.[78] A spokesman for the Houthi-aligned military announced agreement to the ceasefire plan on 10 May, although he warned that a breach of the truce would prompt a military response.[79]

On 13 May, humanitarian agencies said they were trying to get aid into Yemen after a five-day ceasefire took effect on Tuesday night. Ships carrying humanitarian supplies docked at the Houthi-controlled Red Sea port of Hudaydah as planes were standing by to help evacuate the injured.[80] Meanwhile, King Salman doubled his country's Yemen aid pledge to $540 million, funds the UN said would "meet the life-saving and protection needs of 7.5 million people affected".[81]

Airstrikes

At the operation's announcement, coalition leadership stressed that their campaign would attempt a political solution and that they would continue the air and naval blockade.[82] Airstrikes resumed almost immediately following the coalition's announcement of the end of Operation Decisive Storm.[83]

On 22 April airstrikes continued in Taiz, where an army base was hit shortly after Houthi fighters took it over,[84] and Aden, where an airstrike targeted Houthi tanks moving into a contested district,[85] among other locations, such as Al Hudaydah and Ibb.[86] The Houthis continued to fight for territory,[87] with a Houthi spokesman saying the group would be prepared for peace talks on the condition of "a complete halt of attacks". The previous

78 *"Yemen conflict: UN criticises Saudi civilian bombings"*. BBC News. Retrieved 11 May 2015.

79 Fitch, Asa; al-Kibsi, Mohammed (10 May 2015). "Yemen's Houthi Rebels Accept Five-Day Truce Proposal". *The Wall Street Journal*. Retrieved 10 May 2015.

80 Yemen conflict: Aid effort begins as truce takes hold". *BBC News*. 13 May 2015.

81 "Saudi king doubles Yemen aid pledge to $540 mn". *Yahoo! News*. Agence France-Presse. 13 May 2015.

82 "Saudi-led coalition ends military operation in Yemen | News , Middle East | THE DAILY STAR". *www.dailystar.com.lb*.

83 Yemen conflict: Saudis launch new air strikes on rebels". *BBC News*. 23 April 2015.

84 Chappell, Bill (22 April 2015). "Saudi Arabia Shifts Military Campaign in Yemen; Airstrikes Continue". NPR. Retrieved 22 April 2015.

85 *Black, Ian (22 April 2015). "Yemen crisis: air strike hits Aden after Saudi Arabia ends bombing campaign". The Guardian. Retrieved 22 April 2015.*

86 Saudi-led coalition launches air strikes throughout Yemen: residents". *Reuters*. 23 April 2015. Retrieved 23 April 2015.

87 Chappell, Bill (22 April 2015). "Saudi Arabia Shifts Military Campaign in Yemen; Airstrikes Continue". NPR. Retrieved 22 April 2015.

round of UN-sponsored talks collapsed after Houthi rebels attacked Hadi's residence in Sana'a[88]

By 26 April, coalition forces were striking what they described as Houthi military targets in Sana'a and Aden and in other locations, notably in Sa'ada province near the Saudi border, nearly every night.[89] On 26 April, after midnight, airstrikes struck Houthi and pro-Saleh positions and targets in and around Sana'a, Aden, and the Ma'rib and Ad Dali' governorates, backing up anti-Houthi fighters in the latter three locations, with more than 90 rebels reportedly killed.[90] Coalition warships shelled fighters near Aden's commercial port. Saudi warplanes also targeted Houthis in the Sa'dah Governorate, while Saudi artillery fired on targets in the Hajjah Governorate along the border.[91] The Saudi National Guard was deployed on the border.[92]

On 28 April, Sana'a International Airport was bombed[93]by Saudi F-15 fighters to prevent an Iranian plane[94] belonging to Iranian Red Crescent Society (IRCS) from landing, while it was approaching to land. The fighters had warned the plane to turn back, in an unsuccessful attempt to thwart its landing, but the Iranian pilot ignored the "illegal warnings", saying that, on the basis of international law, his plane did not need further permission to land.[95]

On the night of 6 May 2015, the Saudi-led coalition carried out 130 airstrikes in Yemen in a 24-hour period. At first, coalition spokesperson Ahmed Asiri admitted that schools and hospitals were targeted but claimed that these were used as weapon storage sites. Asiri later claimed that his words had been mistranslated. The United Nations humanitarian coordinator for Yemen Johannes Van Der Klaauw said that these bombings constituted a war crime. "The indiscriminate bombing of populated areas, with or without prior warning, is a contravention international humanitarian law," he said. He continued to say that he was particularly concerned about airstrikes on Saada "where scores of civilians were reportedly killed and thousands were forced to flee their homes after the coalition declared the entire governate a military target".[96]

---

88 "Houthis call for peace talks as Saudi planes strike Yemen". CNN. 22 April 2015. Retrieved 22 April 2015.

89 *Air raids and ground clashes rage in Yemen". Al Jazeera. 26 April 2015.*

"Fighting escalates across Yemen, air strikes on capital Sanaa". Reuters. 26 April 2015.

90 "Air raids and ground clashes rage in Yemen". Al Jazeera. 26 April 2015. Retrieved 26 April 2015.

91 Air raids and ground clashes rage in Yemen". Al Jazeera. 26 April 2015. Retrieved 26 April 2015.

92 *"First Saudi National Guards reach Yemen border zone". Al-Ahram. Agence France-Presse. 27 April 2015. Retrieved 27 April 2015*

93 Al-Haj, Ahmed (29 April 2015). "Yemen Rebels and Allies Advance in Southern City of Aden". ABC News. Retrieved 29 April 2015.

94 "Yemen airport bombed". *Reuters*. 29 April 2015. Retrieved 29 April 2015.

95 "Aid flights to Yemen blocked after Saudi Arabian jets bomb airport runway". *The Guardian*. Reuters. 29 April 2015. Retrieved 30 April 2015.

The Iranian Foreign Ministry summoned the Saudi chargé d'affaires, and the Iranian Parliament and the Iranian Red Crescent Society blasted Saudi Arabia for blocking Iranian humanitarian aid.[97]

The UN Office for the Coordination of Humanitarian Affairs (OCHA) "strongly urged" the coalition to stop targeting airports and seaports so that aid could reach all Yemenis.[98]

ICRC and Médecins Sans Frontières (MSF), also known as Doctors Without Borders, said that they were extremely concerned about damage to the airports at Sanaa and to the port city of Hodeidah.[99]

Overnight on 29 and 30 April, SA was reported to have airdropped arms to anti-Houthi fighters in Taiz.[100] Later in the day, the Houthi's announced the death of 1 soldier due to airstrikes on the local police station in Al Bayda, Yemen[101]

On 30 April airstrikes hit five provinces.[102] New airstrikes hit SIA, completely halting aid deliveries.

On 6 May coalition airstrikes targeted the Police Training Center in the Dhamar Governorate, damaging nearby houses[103]meanwhile the civil aviation authority announced it would re-open the airport to receive aid.[104]

Coalition airstrikes targeted the houses of Saleh in Sana'a in the early hours of 10 May, eyewitnesses said. Khabar, a Yemeni news agency allied with Saleh said that the former president and his family were unharmed[105]

---

96 Mariano Castillo (12 May 2015). "U.N. rep accuses Saudi-led coalition of violating international law". CNN.

97 "Iranian Parliament Condemns Saudi Arabia for Blocking Humanitarian Aid to Yemen". ghatreh. Retrieved 18 May 2015.

"Iran Summons Saudi Envoy Over Blocking Humanitarian Aid to Yemen". Kayhan. Retrieved 18 May 2015

98 UN urges Saudi-led coalition to stop targeting Yemen airport". Reuters. 4 May 2015. Retrieved 13 July 2015.

"Humanitarian flights unable to land, after bombing Sana'a International Airport". Yemen Times.

99 "UN urges Saudi-led coalition to stop targeting Yemen airport". Reuters. 4 May 2015. Retrieved 13 July 2015.

100 Heavy fighting in Yemen, Saudi Arabia trains tribal fighters". Reuters. 30 April 2015.

101 Timeline Photos – Almasirah Channel قناة المسيرة -"." – via Facebook

102 Heavy fighting in Yemen, Saudi Arabia trains tribal fighters". Reuters. 30 April 2015.

103 "Saudi airstrikes kill 11 people in Dhamar". Saba News Agency. 6 May 2015. Retrieved 11 May 2015.

104 "Yemen:Saudi-led warplanes bomb Sanaa airport". Retrieved 11 May2015.

105 Saudi air strikes in Yemen target house of ex-president Saleh". The Guardian. 10 May 2015.

The Moroccan government said on 10 May that one of its General Dynamics F-16 Fighting Falcon aircraft taking part in the air campaign went missing in action over Yemen, along with its pilot[106] The Houthis claimed responsibility, with Yemeni state TV broadcasting a report on the jet being downed by tribal militias over the Sa'dah Governorate and showing images of the wreckage.[107]

On 18 May Saudi-led airstrikes reportedly resumed on Houthi positions after a humanitarian ceasefire expired late on Sunday. Three coalition airstrikes hit Sa'ada on Monday. Yemen's exiled Foreign Minister Riyadh Yassin blamed the rebel group for the renewal of hostilities. Al-Arabiya said Saudi forces shelled Houthi outposts along Yemen's northern border after the fighters fired mortars at a Saudi army post in Najran province.[108]

On 23 May OCHA reported that airstrikes continued in the northern governorates of Sa'ada (Baqim, Haydan, Saqayn and As Safra) and Hajjah (Abs, Hayran, Haradh, Huth, Kuhlan Affar and Sahar districts). The road connecting Haradh and Huth districts was reportedly hit. Airstrikes were also reported in Al Jawf Governorate (Bart Al Anan district).[109]

On 27 May airstrikes hit a police station in the capital, Sana'a, killing 45 officers.[110] The Houthi-controlled Ministry of Health announced that in total, 96 people were killed.

On 3 June the residence of a Houthi leader in Ibb province was hit by an airstrike, according to eyewitnesses[111]

On 23 September 2015, the Saudi-led coalition destroyed a ceramics factory in the town of Matnah. One civilian was killed and others were wounded. According to the BBC, the bomb is believed to have been produced in the United Kingdom by GEC-Marconi Dynamics.[112] The factory's owner Ghalib al-Sawary told the BBC: "We built

---

106 "Moroccan Fighter Jet Goes Missing in Yemen". ABC News. 11 May 2015. Retrieved 10 May 2015.

107 Yemen conflict: Houthi rebels 'down Moroccan warplane'". BBC News. 11 May 2015. Retrieved 11 May 2015.

108 "Saudi-led air strikes hit Yemen after truce expires". Reuters. 18 May 2015.

109 "Yemen: Escalating Conflict Flash Update 36" (PDF). ReliefWeb. 23 May 2015. Retrieved 25 February 2016.

110 "Saudi-led airstrikes on Yemen police headquarters kills 45". thehansindia.com. 28 May 2015.

111 "Air strikes kill 20 Houthi fighters in Yemen's Aden: militia". Reuters. 3 June 2015.

112 Orla Guerin (25 March 2016). UK-made bomb 'hit Yemen factory'. BBC News. Retrieved 7 May 2017.

it over 20 years but to destroy it took only twenty minutes."[113] Campaigners say this attack was a violation of the laws of war.

On 26 October 2015 Médecins Sans Frontières reported that a coalition airstrike had completely destroyed a hospital they ran in Saada province's Haydan governorate, including the operating room. When the first strike hit an unused part of the hospital the facility was completely evacuated, so there were no direct casualties. A spokesman for the coalition forces, Brig-Gen Ahmed al-Asiri, denied responsibility for the attack.[114] "With the hospital destroyed, at least 200,000 people now have no access to lifesaving medical care," MSF said. "This attack is another illustration of a complete disregard for civilians in Yemen, where bombings have become a daily routine," said Hassan Boucenine, MSF head of mission in Yemen. The GPS coordinates of the only hospital in the Haydan district were regularly shared with the Saudi-led coalition, and the roof of the facility was clearly identified with the MSF logo, he said.[115] UNICEF said the hospital in Saada was the 39th health center hit in Yemen since March, when the violence escalated. "More children in Yemen may well die from a lack of medicines and healthcare than from bullets and bombs," its executive director Anthony Lake said in a statement. He added that critical shortages of fuel, medication, electricity and water could mean many more will close. Amnesty International said the strike may amount to a war crime and called for an independent investigation[116]

In February 2016, the Saudis bombed the ancient citadel of Kawkaban, killing seven civilians.[117]

On 8 October 2016, Saudi-led airstrikes targeted a hall in Sana'a where a funeral was taking place. At least 140 people were killed and about 600 were wounded. According to *The Independent*, one rescuer said: "The place has been turned into a lake of blood."[118] After initially denying it was behind the attack, the Coalition's Joint Incidents Assessment Team admitted that it had bombed the hall but claimed that this attack had been a mistake caused by bad information.[119] After this attack, US national security spokesperson said that the US government was "deeply disturbed" by the

113 Orla Guerin (26 March 2016). "A year of war that has set Yemen back decades". *BBC News*.

114 "Yemen conflict: MSF hospital destroyed by air strikes". *BBC News*. Retrieved 15 November 2015.

115 "MSF hospital in Yemen bombed by airstrike", Xinhua (28 October 2015)

116 *"Yemeni MSF hospital bombed, Saudi-led coalition denies responsibility"*. *Reuters*. *Retrieved 15 November 2015.*

"Doctors Without Borders says Saudi-led airstrikes bomb Yemen hospital". *Fox News Channel. Retrieved 15 November 2015*

117 Orla Guerin (26 March 2016). "A year of war that has set Yemen back decades". *BBC News*.

118 Ben Kentish (9 October 2016). "Saudi-led coalition in Yemen accused of 'genocide' after airstrike on funeral hall kills 140; US says it will 'review' its support after latest attack". *The Independent*.

119 *"Saudi-led coalition admits to bombing Yemen funeral"*. *The Guardian. 15 October 2016*

bombing and added that US support for the Saudi-led coalition was "not a blank cheque". He added "we have initiated an immediate review of our already significantly reduced support to the Saudi-led Coalition."[120] The United Nations humanitarian co-ordinator in Yemen Jamie McGoldrick said he was "shocked and outraged" by the "horrific" bombing. "This violence against civilians in Yemen must stop," he said[121]

On the night of 15 February 2017, the Saudi-led coalition bombed a funeral reception near Sanaa. Initial reports suggest the bombing killed nine women and one child with ten more women reported wounded. "People heard the sound of planes and started running from the house but then the bombs hit the house directly. The roof collapsed and there was blood was everywhere," a resident of the village told a Reuters news agency cameraman.[122]

An explosion in a warehouse on Sunday 7 April 2019, in Sanaa, have killed at least 11 civilians, including school children and left more than 39 people wounded. The Associated Press news agency said 13 killed, including 7 children and more than 100 were wounded. According to Al Jazeera and Houthi officials, the civilians were killed in a Saudi-led coalition airstrike.[123] The Saudi-led coalition denied any airstrikes took place that day on Sanaa. The state-run news agency in Aden, aligned with the internationally recognized government, said the rebels had stored weapons at the warehouse. According to *The Washington Post*, "some families and residents of the district of Sawan said the explosion occurred after a fire erupted inside the warehouse. They said a fire sent columns of white smoke rising into the air, followed by the explosion." Their accounts were confirmed by several videos filmed by bystanders.[124]

Aircraft losses
List of aviation shootdowns and accidents during the Saudi Arabian-led intervention in Yemen

Cross-border fighting

Saudi Arabian–Yemeni border conflict (2015–present)

---

120 Ben Kentish (9 October 2016). "Saudi-led coalition in Yemen accused of 'genocide' after airstrike on funeral hall kills 140; US says it will 'review' its support after latest attack". *The Independent*.

121 Ben Kentish (9 October 2016). "Saudi-led coalition in Yemen accused of 'genocide' after airstrike on funeral hall kills 140; US says it will 'review' its support after latest attack". *The Independent*.

122 "Air raid on Yemen funeral 'kills at least nine women'; Houthi rebels blame Arab coalition for attack on Shiraa village 40km north of capital Sanaa". Al Jazeera. 16 February 2017.

123 "Saudi-led air raids 'kill at least 11 civilians' in Yemen's Sanaa". aljazeera.com. Aljazeera. 7 April 2019. Retrieved 8 April 2019.

124 *Explosion in Yemen Warehouse Kills at Least 13, Including 7 Children". nytimes.com. Nytimes. 7 April 2019. Retrieved 8 April 2019.*

The Washington Post (8 April 2019). "Yemenis recount horror of mysterious blast in capital"

Ground combat

Battle of Aden (2015); Conflict in Najran, Jizan and Asir; and Battle of Taiz (2015–present)

On 3 April, CNN cited an unnamed Saudi source who claimed that Saudi special forces were on the ground in and around Aden, "coordinating and guiding" the resistance.[125] The Saudi government officially declined to comment on whether it had special forces, with Saudi Ambassador to the United States Adel al-Jubeir saying on 2 April that Saudi Arabia had no "formal" troops in Aden[126]

The Battle of Aden came to an end with pro-Hadi forces again seized control of Aden port and moving into the city's commercial center.[127] On 22 July, pro-Hadi forces had retaken full control of Aden, and the Aden Airport was reopened. In late July, an offensive launched by pro-Hadi forces drove Houthi forces out of the towns neighboring Aden.[128]

On 4 September a Houthi OTR-21 Tochka missile hit an ammunition dump at a military base in Safer in Ma'rib Governorate killing 52 UAE, 10 Saudi and 5 Bahraini soldiers. Coalition forces for a push against Sanaa were building up the Safer base.[129] "It was the deadliest single attack on coalition soldiers since the start of its operation against Houthi rebels in March" Asseri said.[130] The attacked was the highest casualty

---

125 Saudi special forces help oppose Houthi rebels in Yemen, source says". CNN. 3 April 2015. Retrieved 3 April 2015.

126 "Saudi-led airstrikes drive Houthis from Aden". Al Jazeera. 3 April 2015. Retrieved 3 April 2015.

127 Mohammed Mukhashaf (16 July 2015). "Saudi-backed Yemen forces take Aden port from Houthis: residents". Reuters. Retrieved 16 July 2015.

Glen Carey (17 July 2015). "Saudi-Backed Forces in Yemen Claim Victories in Aden Battle". Bloomberg. Retrieved 17 July 2015.

128 "Egypt, Jordan and Sudan ready for ground offensive in Yemen.: report". The Globe and Mail. Toronto. 26 March 2015. Archived from the original on 26 March 2015. Retrieved 26 March 2015.

129 "Yemen crisis: UAE launches fresh Yemen attacks". BBC News. 5 September 2015. Retrieved 6 September 2015.

"Marib province is crucial to coalition victory in Yemen". The National. 7 September 2015. Retrieved 7 September 2015.

"Emirati serviceman dies during Yemen ground offensive". The National. 14 September 2015. Retrieved 14 September 2015.

130 Gray, Melissa (5 September 2015). "Saudi-led coalition strikes back at Houthis". CNN.

loss in the history of the UAE military.[131] Qatar deployed 1000 troops to Yemen after the incident[132]

By 8 September it was reported that the Saudi-led forces deployed in Yemen exceeded 10,000 troops and included 30 AH-64 Apache attack helicopters.[133]

On 14 December media reported a Houthi & Saleh Forces missile attack at a Saudi military camp south-west of the besieged city of Taiz,[134] while sources confirmed the killings of over 150 coalition soldiers including 23 Saudi troops, 9 UAE officers and soldiers, 7 Moroccan soldiers and 42 Blackwater troops.[135]

On 19 December 2015, reported clashes leaves over 40 Houthi rebels and 35 government loyalists dead, with dozens wounded on both sides[136]

In June 2018, anti-Houthi forces led by Saudi Arabia and the United Arab Emirates assaulted the port of Hudaydah,[137] in an effort to dislodge Houthi forces.[138]

131 *"Coalition attacks Yemen capital after UAE, Saudi soldiers killed"*. *Reuters*. Retrieved 15 November 2015

132 Al Jazeera and agencies (7 September 2015). "Qatar deploys 1,000 ground troops to fight in Yemen". Al Jazeera.

133 "Number of Saudi-led coalition troops in Yemen 'rises to 10,000'". *Arabian Business*. Reuters. 8 September 2015. Retrieved 9 September 2015

134 *"Gulf troops dead in Yemen rocket attack, sources"*. alaraby.co.uk. 14 December 2015. Retrieved 8 February 2016.

"Two top Gulf commanders killed in Yemen rocket strike: sources". *Reuters*. 14 December 2015. Retrieved 8 February 2016.

135 *Saudi Coalition, Houthi Rebels Intensify Attacks in Yemen Ahead of Proposed Ceasefire"*. *Financial News*. 14 December 2015. Retrieved 8 February 2016.

^ *"even Moroccan Soldiers Reportedly Killed in Yemen"*. *Morocco World News*. 14 December 2015. Retrieved 8 February 2016.

136 "Fierce Fighting in Yemen kills at Least 75. *Time*.

137 "Arab Coalition Attacks Yemeni City in Bid to Oust Rebels". *The New York Times*. 13 June 2018

138 Nissenbam, Dion. "U.S. Deepens Role in Yemen Fight, Offers Gulf Allies Airstrike-Target Assistance". *The Wall Street Journal*. Archived from the original on 13 June 2018.

Naval involvement
Blockade of Yemen

Estimated fuel needs in Yemen and monthly fuel imports[139]

139 *Yemen: Snapshot on Shipping, Food and Fuel Imports for January 2016 (issued on 13 February 2016)"*. UN Office for the Coordination of Humanitarian Affairs. 13 February 2016. *Archived* from the original on 13 February 2016. (*"PDF"* (PDF). *Archived* from the original on 13 February 2016.)

"Yemen: Reduced Imports Worsen Crisis (as of 5 June 2015)". UN Office for the Coordination of Humanitarian Affairs. 5 June 2015. *Archived* from the original on 6 June 2015.; PDF: *"Yemen: Reduced Imports Worsen Crisis (as of 5 June 2015)"* (PDF). *Archived* from the original on 6 June 2015.

"Yemen: Reduced Imports Worsen Crisis (as of 23 June 2015)". UN Office for the Coordination of Humanitarian Affairs. 23 June 2015. *Archived* from the original on 24 June 2015.; PDF: *"Yemen: Reduced Imports Worsen Crisis (as of 23 June 2015)"* (PDF). *Archived* from the original on 24 June 2015.

"Yemen: Snapshot on Shipping and Food Imports (as of 14 December 2015)". UN Office for the Coordination of Humanitarian Affairs. 14 December 2015. *Archived* from the original on 14 December 2015.; PDF: *"Yemen: Snapshot on Shipping and Food Imports (as of 14 December 2015"* (PDF). *Archived* from the original on 14 December 2015.

Monthly needs (544,000 t)	100%	23%	1%	16%	46%	69%	19%	1%	11%	89%	15%	85%
	Mar 2015	Apr 2015	May 2015	Jun 2015	Jul 2015	Aug 2015	Sep 2015	Oct 2015	Nov 2015	Dec 2015	Jan 2016	

Saudi Arabia faced growing criticism for the Saudi-led naval and air blockade, which effectively isolated the country.[140]

A "military source and pro-Hadi militiamen" told the AFP on 26 April that coalition warships were participating in the shelling of Aden. [141]

On 30 April, the Iranian navy announced it had deployed two destroyers to the Gulf of Aden to "ensure the safety of commercial ships of our country against the threat of pirates", according to a rear admiral.[142] According to the same source, the deployment was scheduled to last until mid-June. Iran's deputy foreign minister, Hossein Amir-Abdollahian, told state-run Tasnim News Agency that "others will not be allowed to put our shared security at risk with military adventures".[143]

Scale and participation of Saudi-led coalition members

Pakistan was called on by Saudi Arabia to join the coalition, but its parliament voted to maintain neutrality.[144] Qatar was suspended from the coalition due to the 2017 Qatar diplomatic crisis[145] Morocco ended their participation in 2019 due to deterioration of Morocco–Saudi Arabia relations[146]followed by United Arab Emirates in July 2019 amid possible tensions with Iran on the Persian Gulf and differences with Saudi Arabia. [4] Sudan announced its decision to reduce troops commitment from 15,000 to 5,000 in early December 2019.[147]

---

140 Kalfood, Mohammed Ali; Fahim, Kareem (12 May 2015). "A Cease-Fire in Yemen, but Fighting Is Persistent". The New York Times. Archived from the original on 29 December 2015. ((Printed version: The New York Times, 13 May 2015, page A10 of the New York edition)).

141 "Clashes rage in Yemen as calls for peace talks grow". Yahoo! News. Agence France-Presse. 26 April 2015.

142 "Iran says warships at entrance to key Yemen strait". Yahoo! News. Agence France-Presse. 30 April 2015.

143 "Iran pledges to protect shared security interests with Yemen -Tasnim". Reuters. 2 May 2015. Retrieved 2 May 2015.

144 "Parliament passes resolution for neutrality in Yemen conflict – PAKISTAN – geo.tv". 10 April 2015. Retrieved 15 April 2015.

145 ANI (5 June 2017). "Gulf rift deepens: Saudi suspends Qatar troops' involvement in Yemen war". Business Standard. Retrieved 30 October 2017

146 "Sudan says it has reduced troops in Yemen to 5,000". Reuters. 8 December 2019 – via uk.reuters.com.

147 Sudan says it has reduced troops in Yemen to 5,000". Reuters. 8 December 2019 – via uk.reuters.com.

Reports of war crimes

Human rights violations during the Yemeni Civil War (2015–present) and Blockade of Yemen

Airstrikes in Yemen apparently violating the laws of war (selection)
HRWinvestigation of 10 Saudi-led coalition airstrikes, that took place between 11 April and 30 August 2015. HRW found either no evident military target or the attack failed to distinguish civilians from military objectives, in apparent violation of the laws of war.[148]

date (in 2015)	location / governorate	objectives or targets struck	civilians killed (at least)				civilians injured
			men	women	children	total	
11 April	Amran / Amran	buildings in the town	1	2	1	4	1
12 May	Abs / Hajjah	Abs/Kholan Prison and other buildings in the town	21	1	3	25	18
12 May	Zabid / Al Hudaydah	Shagia market and lemon grove in the town	39	13	8	60	155

---

148 *"What Military Target Was in My Brother's House – Unlawful Coalition Airstrikes in Yemen"*. *Human Rights Watch. 26 November 2015. Archivedfrom the original on 27 November 2015. ("PDF download" (PDF). Archived from the original on 27 November 2015.)*

4 July	Muthalith Ahim / Al Hudaydah	marketplace in the village	?	?	3	65	105
6 July	Amran	1. Bawn market between Amran und Raydah; 2. Jawb market outside the town	13	1	15	29	20
12	Sana'a-	*muhamashee* resident	2	7	14	23	31

July	Sawan / San a'a	ial neighborhood					people
19 July	Yarim / Ibb	residential homes and buildings in the town	4	3	9	16	16
24	Mokha / Taiz	residential compound	42	13	10	65	55

July		of Mokha Steam Power Plant					
8 August	Shara'a / Ibb	homes in the village (Radhma district)	2	3	3	8	2

30 August	Abs / Hajjah	Al-Sham Water Bottling Factory in the outskirts of the town	11		3	14	11
civilian airstrike casualties for all 10 airstrikes, investigated by HRW (report of 26 November 2015)			**309**				**414**

The Saudi-led campaign has received widespread criticism and had a dramatic worsening effect on the humanitarian situation in Yemen, that reached the level of a "humanitarian disaster"[21] or "humanitarian catastrophe".[149]After the Saudi-led coalition declared the entire Saada Governorate a military target, the UN's Humanitarian Coordinator for Yemen and Human Rights Watch expressed concern that the bombing there was unnecessarily harming civilians.[251][252] On 1 July UN declared for Yemen a "level-three" emergency—the highest UN emergency level—for a period of six months.[253] [254] Human rights groups repeatedly blamed the Saudi-led military coalition for killing civilians and destroying health centres and other infrastructure with airstrikes.[255] The de facto blockade left 78% (20 million) of the Yemeni population in urgent need of food, water and medical aid. Aid ships are allowed, but the bulk of commercial shipping, on which the country relies, is blocked.[256] In one incident, coalition jets prevented an Iranian Red Crescent plane from landing by bombing Sana'a International Airport's runway, which blocked aid delivery by air.[257] As of 10 December, more than 2,500,000 people had been internally displaced by the fighting.[258] Many countries evacuated more than 23,000 foreign citizens from Yemen.[150] More than 1,000,000 people fled Yemen for Saudi Arabia, [262] Djibouti, Somalia, Ethiopia, Sudan and Oman[151]The war has caused a humanitarian

---

149 _"Durable ceasefire needed as 'humanitarian catastrophe' leaves millions suffering in Yemen – UN relief chief)"_. UN News Centre. 28 July 2015. _Archived_ from the original on 29 July 2015.

"European Commission steps up humanitarian aid for Yemen crisis". European Commission's Directorate-General for European Civil Protection and Humanitarian Aid Operations. 14 December 2015. _Archived_ from the original on 17 December 2015 – via _ReliefWeb_.; Original source: _"European Commission steps up humanitarian aid for Yemen crisis"_. 14 December 2015. _Archived_ from the original on 17 December 2015.

"Yemen crisis: How bad is the humanitarian situation?". BBC News. 24 August 2015. _Archived_ from the original on 28 September 2015.

150 Kumar, Hari; Barry, Ellen (5 April 2015). _"India Tries Evacuating Citizens in Yemen"_. _The New York Times_.

"Yemen crisis: China evacuates citizens and foreigners from Aden". BBC News. 3 April 2015.

b _"Regional refugee and Migrant Response: Impact of the Yemen Crisis, 15 December 2015 [EN/ AR]"_. International Organization for Migration, UN High Commissioner for Refugees. 15 December 2015. _Archived_ from the original on 29 December 2015 – via _ReliefWeb_.; PDF: _"Regional refugee and Migrant Response: Impact of the Yemen Crisis, 15 December 2015 [EN/AR]"_ (PDF). _Archived_ from the original on 29 December 2015.

151 Kumar, Hari; Barry, Ellen (5 April 2015). _"India Tries Evacuating Citizens in Yemen"_. _The New York Times_.

crisis, including a famine which has threatened over 17 million people, as well as an outbreak of cholera which has infected hundreds of thousands.

On 13 April 2015, HRW wrote that some airstrikes were in apparent violation of the laws of war, such as 30 March attack on a displaced-persons camp in Mazraq that struck a medical facility and a market.[263] Other incidents noted by HRW that had been deemed as indiscriminate or disproportionate or "in violation of the laws of war" were: a strike on a dairy factory outside the Red Sea port of Hodaida (31 civilian deaths);[264] a strike that destroyed a humanitarian aid warehouse of the international aid organization Oxfam in Saada;[265] and the coalition's blockade that kept out fuel.[266] On 30 June 2015, HRW reported that several airstrikes were in clear violation of international law. The report confirmed 59 (including 14 women and 35 children) civilian deaths in Saada between 6 April and 11 May. The report also highlighted attacks on 6 civilian homes as well as five markets that were deliberate attacks.[152]

In February 2016, Amnesty International (AI) reported that it had investigated the circumstances and impact of more than 30 air strikes of the Saudi Arabia-led coalition forces in Sana'a, Hodeidah, Hajjah and Sa'da. They believed that the coalition was intentionally striking civilian targets.[268] On 24 April 2015, Amnesty International said that airstrikes hit five densely populated areas (Sa'dah, Sana'a, Hodeidah, Hajjah and Ibb), and "raise concerns about compliance with the rules of international humanitarian law."[269] [270] Their research indicates that there were at least 97 civilian deaths, including 33 children, and 157 civilians were wounded.[269]

According to Farea Al-Muslim, direct war crimes were committed during the conflict; for example, an IDP(Internally displaced person) camp was hit by a Saudi airstrike, while Houthis sometimes prevented aid workers from giving aid.[271] The UN and human rights groups discussed the possibility that war crimes may have been committed by Saudi Arabia during the air campaign.[272]

US Representative Ted Lieu has criticized the Saudi-led attacks on Yemen: "Some of these strikes look like war crimes to me, and I want to get answers as to why the US appears to be assisting in the execution of war crimes in Yemen."[273]

In March 2017, Human Rights Watch (HRW) reported that "Since the start of the current conflict, at least 4,773 civilians had been killed and 8,272 wounded, the majority by coalition airstrikes.... Human Rights Watch has documented 62 apparently unlawful coalition airstrikes, some of which may amount to war crimes, that have killed nearly 900 civilians, and documented seven indiscriminate attacks by Houthi-Saleh forces in Aden and Taizz that killed 139 people, including at least eight children."[274]

In an April 2020 report, the Human Rights Watch pointed out that the war crimes committed by Saudi Arabia and United Arab Emirates in Yemen go unmentioned. The countries have been held responsible for most number of child casualties and illegal attacks on schools.[153]

2. ^ "Yemen crisis: China evacuates citizens and foreigners from Aden". BBC News. 3 April 2015.

"Regional refugee and Migrant Response: Impact of the Yemen Crisis, 15 December 2015 [EN/AR]". International Organization for Migration, UN High Commissioner for Refugees. 15 December 2015. Archived from the original on 29 December 2015 – via ReliefWeb.; PDF: "Regional refugee and Migrant Response: Impact of the Yemen Crisis, 15 December 2015 [EN/AR]" (PDF). Archived from the original on 29 December 2015.

152 "Saudi airstrikes in Yemen violate laws of war, rights group says". McClatchy DC. Retrieved 13 July 2015.

153 The UN's Timid Responses to War Crimes Against Children". Human Rights Watch. Retrieved 10 April 2020.

Declaring the entire governorate of Sa'ada a military target

On 8 May 2015, a spokesperson for the Saudi-led coalition declared the entire city of Sa'dah, with a population of around 50,000 people, a military target. According to Human Rights Watch: "This not only violated the laws-of-war prohibition against placing civilians at particular risk by treating a number of separate and distinct military objectives as a single military target, but possibly also the prohibition against making threats of violence whose purpose is to instill terror in the civilian population."[276]

Human Rights Watch compiled the names and ages of some of the people killed in Saada City between 6 April and 11 May. Of the 59 people they found information on, 35 were children and 14 were women.[276] The organisation's analysis of air-strike locations in Sa'dah showed that bombs fell across the city including near markets, schools and hospitals.[276]

U.N. Humanitarian Coordinator for Yemen, Johannes van der Klaauw, agreed that the Saud-led coalition's actions breached international humanitarian law.[251][252] "The indiscriminate bombing of populated areas, with or without prior warning, is in contravention of international humanitarian law," he said.[191] He added that he was concerned that "scores of civilians were reportedly killed and thousands were forced to flee their homes after the coalition declared the entire governate a military target."

Save the Children's Country Director in Yemen, Edward Santiago, said that the "indiscriminate attacks after the dropping of leaflets urging civilians to leave Sa'ada raises concerns about the possible pattern being established in breach of International Humanitarian Law. Warning civilians does not exonerate the coalition from their obligation to protect civilians and civilian infrastructure, and we have seen in the last days that the warnings have not been enough to spare civilian lives. At the same time, people are largely unable to flee for safety because of the de facto blockade imposed by the coalition leading to severe fuel shortages."[277]

Attacks on facilities run by aid organizations

Since the Saudi-led coalition began military operations against Ansar Allah on 26 March 2015, Saudi-led coalition airstrikes unlawfully struck hospitals and other facilities run by aid organizations, according to Human Rights Watch.[278] Médecins Sans Frontières (MSF) medical facilities in Yemen were attacked four times in three months. [279] On 26 October 2015, HRW documented six Saudi-led airstrikes which bombed a MSF hospital in Haydan district (Sa'dah Governorate), wounding two patients.[278][279][280] A Saudi-led coalition airstrike then hit a MSF mobile clinic on 2 December 2015, in Al Houban district (Taizz). Eight people were wounded, including two MSF staff members, and one other civilian nearby was killed. On 10 January 2016, six people were killed and seven wounded when a hospital in Sa'ada was hit by a projectile.[278][279] MSF said it could not confirm whether the hospital was hit in an air strike by warplanes of the Saudi-led coalition, or by a rocket fired from the ground, and at least one other landed nearby.[278] [281] On 21 January 2016, an MSF ambulance was hit by an airstrike. Seven people were killed and dozens were wounded.[278][279]

MSF's director of operations Raquel Ayora said: "The way war is being waged in Yemen is causing enormous suffering and shows that the warring parties do not recognise or respect the protected status of hospitals and medical facilities. We witness the devastating consequences of this on people trapped in conflict zones on a daily basis. Nothing has been spared—not even hospitals, even though medical facilities are explicitly protected by international humanitarian law."[279]

The Saudi embassy in London, in early February 2016, advised United Nations and other aid organizations to move their offices and staff away from "regions where the Houthi militias and their supporters are active and in areas where there are military operations". It claimed this was in order to "protect the international organizations and their employees".[278] The UN refused to pull out the humanitarian aid workers and protested against the Saudi demands.[154] On 7 February 2016, the UN humanitarian chief Stephen O'Brien wrote to Saudi Arabia's UN Ambassador Abdallah al-Mouallimi, pointing out that Saudi Arabia is obligated under international law to permit access, and has "duty of care obligations under the conduct of military operations for all civilians, including humanitarian workers".[278]

HRW declared, on 17 February 2016, that Saudi Arabia's warnings to stay away were insufficient to fulfil their legal obligations to protect aid stations and their occupants. James Ross, Legal and Policy Director at HRW, said: "A warning is no justification for an unlawful airstrike. They can't shift the blame for shirking their responsibility onto aid agencies that are struggling to address a deepening crisis."[278]

After an air-strike on an MSF hospital in the Hajjah province on 15 August 2016, MSF announced the pulling of their staff from Saada and Hajjah provinces affecting 6 facilities. The group also complained that the results of previous investigations into hospital bombings by the Saudi-led coalition were never shared.[284]

Usage of cluster munitions

In early May 2015, Human Rights Watch accused Saudi Arabia of using US-supplied cluster munitions on at least two occasions. The Saudi military acknowledged using CBU-105 bombs, but it claimed they were only employed against armoured vehicles and not in population centers.[285][286] Yemeni security officials claimed that cluster bombs were dropped in a civilian area of the Western suburbs of the Yemeni capital Sanaa. In an earlier statement, Saudi Arabia had denied that the Saudi-led military coalition was using cluster bombs at all.[215]

Internationally outlawed cluster bombs supplied by the USA were used by the Saudi-led military coalition and wounded civilians despite evidence of prior civilian casualties, based on multiple reports issued by HRW.[287]

On 8 January 2016, the UN Secretary General Ban Ki-moon announced that Saudi coalition use of cluster munitions could be a war crime.[155] HRW condemned the Saudi-led coalition for the attacks saying: "The coalition's repeated use of cluster bombs in the middle of a crowded city suggests an intent to harm civilians, which is a war crime. These outrageous attacks show that the coalition seems less concerned than ever about [156]sparing civilians from war's horrors."[157] A week later, Amnesty International published

---

154 Hackwill, Robert (17 February 2016). _"Yemen struggles to see way out of war"_. euronews.com. Archived from the original on 20 February 2016.

"Wegen Jemen-Krieg: Kontroverse zwischen Saudi-Arabien und UN" (in German). de.euronews.com. 17 February 2016. Archived from the original on 18 February 2016

155 Charbonneau, Louis (8 January 2016). _"Use of cluster bombs in Yemen may be war crime: U.N. chief"_. Reuters. Archived from the original on 10 January 2016.

156 _"Yemen: Coalition Drops Cluster Bombs in Capital – Indiscriminate Weapon Used in Residential Areas"_. Human Rights Watch. 7 January 2016. Archived from the original on 7 January 2016.

157 _"Yemen: Coalition Drops Cluster Bombs in Capital – Indiscriminate Weapon Used in Residential Areas"_. Human Rights Watch. 7 January 2016. Archived from the original on 7 January 2016.

new evidence that appeared to confirm reports of coalition forces using US-made cluster munitions on Sana'a on 6 January 2016.[158]

In December 2016, a Saudi spokesperson admitted that at least some of the coalition's cluster bombs were manufactured in the United Kingdom. British prime minister Theresa May refused to answer when asked in parliament when she first became aware that UK-made cluster bombs were being used.[292]

Amnesty International has called on Saudi Arabia to destroy its stockpile of cluster bombs and accede to the International Convention on Cluster Munitions. It also asked the Saudi-led coalition to provide the United Nations with precise locations of cluster munition attacks.[159] The coalition has yet to do so.

In May 2019, Saudi Arabia's cargo ship Bahri-Yanbu was blocked from collecting weapons at the French Port of Le Havre by humanitarian groups. Later in the month, Italian union workers refused to load electricity generators on the ship and prevented it from docking, claiming that the weapons on-board would be used against civilians. Despite the protests, the ship docked.[160]

---

158 *"Yemen: New evidence challenges coalition's denial it used cluster munitions in recent attack (Index number: MDE 31/3208/2016)"*. *Amnesty International. 15 January 2016. Archived from the original on 16 January 2016. ("PDF"(PDF). Archived from the original on 16 January 2016., "original PDF"(PDF). Archived from the original on 16 January 2016.)*

159 Saudi Arabia: Immediately abandon all use of cluster munitions". Amnesty International. 19 December 2016.

160 "Italian unions refuse to load Saudi ship carrying weapons to Yemen". Euronews. 21 May 2019. Retrieved 21 May 2019.

Calls for international independent investigations

A UN panel of experts said in a report for the UN Security Council in January 2016, which was leaked to *The Guardian*, that the Saudi-led coalition had undertaken 119 sorties in Yemen that violated international humanitarian law.[161] The panel said it had "documented that the coalition had conducted airstrikes targeting civilians and civilian objects, in violation of international humanitarian law, including camps for internally displaced persons and refugees; civilian gatherings, including weddings; civilian vehicles, including buses; civilian residential areas; medical facilities; schools; mosques; markets, factories and food storage warehouses; and other essential civilian infrastructure, such as the airport in Sana'a, the port in Hudaydah and domestic transit routes". The report said: "Many attacks involved multiple airstrikes on multiple civilian objects. Of the 119 sorties, the panel identified 146 targeted objects. The panel also documented three alleged cases of civilians fleeing residential bombings and being chased and shot at by helicopters."[162] While the UN experts were not allowed on the ground in Yemen, they studied satellite imagery of cities before and after attacks, that showed "extensive damage to residential areas and civilian objects".[163]The UN panel concluded that "civilians are disproportionately affected" by the fighting and deplored tactics that "constitute the prohibited use of starvation as a method of warfare".[164]The report said: "The coalition's targeting of civilians through airstrikes, either by bombing residential neighbourhoods or by treating the entire cities of Sa'dah and Maran as military targets, is a grave violation of the principles of distinction, proportionality and precaution. In certain cases, the panel found such violations to have been conducted in a widespread and systematic manner."[165] The report called for an international commission, set up by the Security Council, that should "investigate reports of violations of international humanitarian law and human rights law in Yemen by all parties and to identify the perpetrators of such violations".[166]Saudi Arabia had previously objected to an inquiry being set up.[167]

---

161 UN Panel Alleges Violations of International Law in Yemen". Voice of America. 26 January 2016. Archived from the original on 28 January 2016

162 MacAskill, Ewen (27 January 2016). "UN report into Saudi-led strikes in Yemen raises questions over UK role – Experts conclude Saudi-led coalition conducted widespread airstrikes against civilian targets in violation of international law". *The Guardian*. Archived from the original on 28 January 2016.

163 UN Panel Alleges Violations of International Law in Yemen". Voice of America. 26 January 2016. Archived from the original on 28 January 2016.

164 MacAskill, Ewen (27 January 2016). "UN report into Saudi-led strikes in Yemen raises questions over UK role – Experts conclude Saudi-led coalition conducted widespread airstrikes against civilian targets in violation of international law". *The Guardian*. Archived from the original on 28 January 2016.

165 *"UN Panel Alleges Violations of International Law in Yemen". Voice of America. 26 January 2016. Archived from the original on 28 January 2016.*

166 MacAskill, Ewen (27 January 2016). "UN report into Saudi-led strikes in Yemen raises questions over UK role – Experts conclude Saudi-led coalition conducted widespread airstrikes against civilian targets in violation of international law". *The Guardian*. Archived from the original on 28 January 2016.

167 *Statement by Adama Dieng, Special Adviser on the Prevention of Genocide and Jennifer Welsh, Special Adviser on the Responsibility to Protect, on the situation in Yemen (16 February 2016)". ReliefWeb. 16 February 2016. Archived from the original on 17 February 2016. ("Statement by Adama Dieng, Special Adviser on the Prevention of Genocide and Jennifer Welsh, Special Adviser on the Responsibility to Protect, on the situation in Yemen"(PDF) (Press*

Five days after the release of UN Panel of Experts report on Yemen, on 31 January 2016, the Saudi-led Arab coalition announced it had formed "an independent team of experts in international humanitarian law and weapons to assess the incidents and investigate the rules of engagement". The coalition said the objective was to "develop a clear and comprehensive report on each incident with the conclusions, lessons learned, recommendations and measures that should be taken" to spare civilians.[168]

On 16 February 2016, Adama Dieng, the U.N.'s Special Adviser on the Prevention of Genocide, and Jennifer Welsh, the Special Adviser on the Responsibility to Protect, said in a joint statement: "We now expect that commitments by the Yemeni authorities and by Saudi Arabia to conduct credible and independent investigations into all alleged violations and provide reparations to victims will be swiftly implemented. It is imperative that the international community also gives immediate consideration to the most effective means of supporting this goal, including the possibility of establishing an international independent and impartial mechanism to support accountability in Yemen."[169]

Alleged use of white phosphorus

In September 2016, *The Washington Post* reported that Saudi Arabia "appears" to be using US-made white phosphorus munitions against Yemen, based on images and videos posted to social media. Under US regulations, white phosphorus is only allowed to be used to signal to other troops and to reduce visibility in open ground, creating a smoke-screen. It is not to be used to attack humans as it burns human flesh down to the bone, which is considered excessively cruel. A United States official said the department was looking into whether the Saudis used white phosphorus improperly[170]

UAE secret prisons

In October 2017, A Yemeni citizen died under "severe torture" inside a secret prison run by the United Arab Emirates in the south of Yemen. As videos showed, the body of Ahmed Dubba revealed disturbing signs of torture after it was released from Khanfar Prison. According to media reports, UAE forces in Yemen had carried out a detention campaign against religious scholars and preachers who opposed their presence in the country where prisoners were subject to physical and psychological torture. According to Yemeni rights group Sam, the issue of secret prisons in Yemen has become a regular phenomenon.[171]

release). United Nations. 16 February 2016. Archived from the original on 17 February 2016.)

168 "Saudi-led Yemen coalition announces probe into possible abuses". Reliefweb. Agence France-Presse. 31 January 2016. Archived from the original on 31 January 2016.

169 Statement by Adama Dieng, Special Adviser on the Prevention of Genocide and Jennifer Welsh, Special Adviser on the Responsibility to Protect, on the situation in Yemen (16 February 2016)". ReliefWeb. 16 February 2016. Archived from the original on 17 February 2016. ("Statement by Adama Dieng, Special Adviser on the Prevention of Genocide and Jennifer Welsh, Special Adviser on the Responsibility to Protect, on the situation in Yemen"(PDF) (Press release). United Nations. 16 February 2016. Archived from the original on 17 February 2016.)

170 Thomas Gibbons-Neff (19 September 2016). "Saudi Arabia appears to be using U.S.-supplied white phosphorus in its war in Yemen". The Washington Post.

171 "Yemeni dies of torture in UAE run prison in Yemen". Middle East Monitor. 30 September 2017.

Targeting of wounded and medical personnel

The United Nations alleged that the Saudi-led coalition had committed a war crime[172]because the bombing was a 'double tap' attack. This is when a second one soon after, which aims to attack the wounded, aid workers, follows the first bombing and medical personnel tending to them. The UN report said: "The second air strike, which occurred three to eight minutes after the first air strike, almost certainly resulted in more casualties to the already wounded and the first responders."[173] Saudi Foreign Minister Adel al-Jubeir said that his government was being careful to abide by humanitarian law.[174]

According to the Save the Children group, children have died as a result of Saudi Arabia delaying aid for Yemen by month.[175]

Use of child soldiers

On late March 2019 the British newspaper *The Mail on Sunday* reported that British Special Forces are fighting on the same side as jihadists and militia which use child soldiers.[303] After the report, The shadow foreign secretary Emily Thornberry, questioned these allegations in the British parliament suggesting that the British forces may have been witnesses to war crimes, if the allegations were true. She claimed that as many as 40% of the soldiers in the Saudi coalition were children, a breach of international humanitarian law[176] In response, the UK Foreign Office minister Mark Field called the allegations "very serious and well sourced" and promised to get to the bottom of these allegations.[304]

In April 2019 the Qatari-based news agency Aljazeera, reported, based in footage of the presence of child soldiers in the recruitment camps of the Saudi-UAE-led coalition. Children from 15 to 16 were recruited from poverty driven Yemeni villages.[177]

Foreign involvement [

NATO powers such as the United Kingdom and the United States support the Saudi Arabian-led intervention in Yemen primarily through arms sales and technical assistance.[306] France had also made recent military sales to Saudi Arabia.[307] MSF emergency coordinator Karline Kleijer called the US, France and the UK part of the Saudi-led coalition, which imposed the weapons embargo and blocked all ships from entering Yemen with supplies.[178] Rights groups have criticized the countries for supplying arms,

172   Michelle Nichols (20 October 2016). "Saudi coalition violated law with Yemen funeral strike: U.N. monitors". Reuters.

173   Michelle Nichols (20 October 2016). "Saudi coalition violated law with Yemen funeral strike: U.N. monitors". Reuters.

174   Michelle Nichols (20 October 2016). "Saudi coalition violated law with Yemen funeral strike: U.N. monitors". Reuters.

175   Samuel Osborne (1 March 2017). "Saudi Arabia delaying aid to Yemen is 'killing children', warns Save the Children; Saudi-led coalition accused of 'turning aid and commercial supplies into weapons of war'". The Independent.

176   editor, Patrick Wintour Diplomatic (27 March 2019). "'Serious' questions over SAS involvement in Yemen war". The Guardian. ISSN 0261-3077. Retrieved 30 March 2019.

177   Exclusive: Yemeni child soldiers recruited by Saudi-UAE coalition". www.aljazeera.com.

178   Kleijer, Karline (9 November 2015). "Yemen: 'The children have a game called airstrike in which they fall to the ground'". The Guardian. Archivedfrom the original on 11 November 2015.

and accuse the coalition of using cluster munitions, which are banned in most countries.[179] Oxfam pointed out that Germany, Iran, and Russia have also reportedly sold arms to the conflicting forces.[180] Tariq Riebl, head of programmes in Yemen for Oxfam, said, "it's difficult to argue that a weapon sold to Saudi Arabia would not in some way be used in Yemen," or "if it's not used in Yemen it enables the country to use other weapons in Yemen."[181] Amnesty International urged the US and the UK to stop supplying arms to Saudi Arabia and to the Saudi-led coalition.[182] On August 3, 2019, a United Nations report said the US, UK and France may be complicit in committing war crimes in Yemen by selling weapons and providing support to the Saudi-led coalition which is using the deliberate starvation of civilians as a tactic of warfare[183]

Overall airstrike casualties[

Year	Date	Place	Deaths	Source
2015	26 March – 7 April[184]	Sana'a	88 civilians	U.N.

179 Nichols, Michelle (22 December 2015). "U.N. blames Saudi-led coalition for most attacks on Yemeni civilians". *Reuters UK*. Archived from the original on 24 December 2015

180 *"UK arms sales fuelling Yemen crisis in potential breach of law says Oxfam"*. Oxfam UK. 11 September 2015. Archived from the original on 30 January 2016.

181 Gatehouse, Gabriel (11 September 2015). "Inside Yemen's forgotten war". *BBC News*. Archived from the original on 1 November 2015.

182 *Sandhu, Serina (8 October 2015). "Amnesty International urges Britain to stop supplying arms to Saudi Arabia – Airstrikes in Yemen have killed thousands of civilians". The Independent*. Archived from the original on 22 November 2015.

183 *"UN Report on Yemen: US, UK Accomplices to Atrocities, While Inaction Continues". The Real News*. 4 September 2019. Retrieved 4 September2019.

Wintour, Patrick (3 September 2019). *"UK, US and France may be complicit in Yemen war crimes – UN report". The Guardian*. Retrieved 4 September2019.

184 Yemen: Escalating Conflict Flash Update 6" (PDF). United Nations Office for the Coordination of Humanitarian Affairs. 8 April 2015. Retrieved 10 June2017.

201 5	26 March – 23 April[185]	Sana'a	209 people	U.N.
201 5	30 March[186]	Mazraq	29 civilians	U.N.
201 5	31 March[187]	Saada	19 civilians	U.N.
201 5	31 March[188]	Ibb province	14 people (11 civilians)	Local sources
201 5	31 March[189]	Wadi Saan	10 civilians	Local sources
201 5	31 March[190]	Hodeida governorate	31 civilians	HRW
201 5	4 April[191]	Sanaa governorate	9 civilians of the same family	Reuters via Local sources

185 Yemen violence death toll tops 1,000: UN". Agence France-Presse. 23 April 2015. Retrieved 26 April 2015.

186 "Letter to US Secretary of Defense Ashton Carter on Armed Conflict in Yemen". Human Rights Watch. 13 April 2015. Retrieved 11 May 2015.

187 Ahmed Al-Haj. "Yemen civilian casualties alarm UN as Saudi-led airstrikes pound rebels". Toronto Star. Associated Press. Retrieved 1 April 2015.

188 "Decisive Storm arrives in Ibb, killing 14 and injuring dozens". Yemen Times. Archived from the original on 3 April 2015. Retrieved 7 April 2020.

189 "Deadly bombings strike private cement company in Lahj". Yemen Times

190 "Yemen: Factory Airstrike Killed 31 Civilians". Human Rights Watch. 16 April 2015. Retrieved 11 May 2015.

191 Yemen air strike kills family of nine: residents". Reuters. 4 April 2015.

2015	7 April[192]	Maitam	3 civilians	Local sources
2015	12 April[193]	Taiz	8 civilians	Local sources
2015	14 April[194]	Taiz	10 civilians	Amnesty International
2015	17 April[195]	Yarim, south of Sanaa	7 civilians	Local sources
2015	17 April[196]	Sanaa	8 civilians	
2015	18 April[197]	Saada	1 civilian	Local sources
2015	19–29 April[198]	Haradh	15 people	U.N.

---

192 Nima Elbagir; Don Melvin (7 April 2015). "Yemen: Saudi airstrike hit school". CNN.

"Warplanes hit Houthi base in central Yemen, students reported killed". Reuters India. 7 April 2015.

193 Yemen's exiled president appoints conciliatory figure as deputy". Reuters. 12 April 2015. Retrieved 15 April 2015.

194 "Yemen: 'nowhere safe for civilians': airstrikes and ground attacks in yemen". Retrieved 14 October 2015.

195 "Yemeni Man Saw Family Burn in Saudi Airstrike". Sky News. Retrieved 26 April 2015.

196 Tadros, Sherine (17 April 2015). "Yemeni Man Saw Family Burn in Saudi Airstrike". Sky News. Retrieved 18 May 2015.

197 Yemen: Warehouse Strike Threatens Aid Delivery". Human Rights Watch. 23 April 2015.

198 Yemen: Escalating Conflict Flash Update 21 – 29 April 2015". UN Office for the Coordination of Humanitarian Affairs. 29 April 2015. Archivedfrom the original on 16 May 2015. ("PDF" (PDF). Archived from the original on 16 May 2015.)

201 5	20 April[199]	Fajj Atan military base, Sana'a	90 people	ICRC
201 5	21 April–5 May[200]	Aden	22 civilians	U.N.
201 5	21 April[201]	Ibb province	20 people	Local sources
201 5	21 April[202]	Haradh	9 people	Local sources
201 5	26 April[203]	Al-Thawra hospital, Taiz	19 people	U.N.
201 5	27 April[334]	Aden	2 civilians	Local sources
201 5	27–28 April[204]	Bajel District	30 people	U.N.
201 5	28 April[205]	between Al-Qaras and Basatir	40 civilians	Local sources

199 "Life under siege in Yemen: 'Bullets and shrapnel came into the house'". *The Guardian*.

200 "Yemen:Saudi-led warplanes bomb Sanaa airport". Retrieved 11 May2015.

201 Winter, Michael (21 April 2015). "Saudis halt bombing of Houthi rebels in Yemen". *USA Today*. Retrieved 22 April 2015.

202 Winter, Michael (21 April 2015). "Saudis halt bombing of Houthi rebels in Yemen". *USA Today*. Retrieved 22 April 2015.

203 "Yemen crisis: Death toll close to 1,250 as Russia attacks UN Security Council for 'amazing indecision'". ABC News.

204 "Yemen: Escalating Conflict Flash Update 20" (PDF). ReliefWeb. Retrieved 10 June 2017.

205 *"Forty Somali refugees killed by Saudi-led bombing campaign in Yemen"*. *Goobjoog. 28 April 2015. Retrieved 28 April 2015.*

201 5	1 May[206]	Sana'a	17 civilians	U.N.
201 5	6 May[207]	Sadaa	34 people including at least 27 civilians	U.N. and HRW
201 5	6 May[208]	Sanaa	20 people	U.N.
201 5	6 May[209]	Kitaf	7 civilians	Local sources
201 5	6 May[210]	Dhamar governorate	11 people	Local sources
201 5	9 May[211]	Saada	4 civilians	U.N.
201 5	11 May[212]	Sanaa	5 people	Agence France-Presse

206 *"Yemen conflict death toll nears 650, with UN rights office spotlighting plight of 3 million disabled"*. UN News Centre. 5 May 2015. Archived from the original on 8 May 2015.

207 Yemen: Escalating Conflict Flash Update 27" (PDF). ReliefWeb. 7 May 2015. Retrieved 25 February 2016.
Dispatches: Renewed Fighting in Yemen Should Not Mean Renewed Violations". Human Rights Watch. 18 May 2015.

208 Yemen: Escalating Conflict Flash Update 27" (PDF). ReliefWeb. 7 May 2015. Retrieved 25 February 2016.

209 "Yemen war: Saudi-led air strike on bus kills 29 children". *BBC News*. 9 August 2018.

210 "Saudi airstrikes kill 11 people in Dhamar". Saba News Agency. 6 May 2015. Retrieved 11 May 2015.

211 Yemen: Escalating Conflict Flash Update 29" (PDF). United Nations Office for the Coordination of Humanitarian Affair. 9 May 2015.

212 Blasts shake Yemen capital as coalition hits arms depot". *GlobalPost*. Retrieved 18 May 2015.

2015	14 May[213]	Saada	9 people	Associated Press
2015	21 May[214]	Hajjah Governorate	5 civilians	U.N
2015	26 May[215]	Saada	7 civilians	Local sources
2015	26 May[216]	Taiz	8 civilians	Amnesty International
2015	27 May[217]	Saada and Yemen	80–100 people	Reuters
2015	4 June[218]	Across Yemen	58 people	Local sources
2015	6 June[219]	Across Yemen	38 people	Local sources

213 Onyanga-Omara, Jane (14 May 2015). "Reports: Yemen airstrike kills 9 amid cease-fire". USA Today. Retrieved 18 May 2015.

214 "Yemen: Escalating Conflict Flash Update 35 – 21 May 2015". UN Office for the Coordination of Humanitarian Affairs. 21 May 2015. Archivedfrom the original on 22 May 2015. (PDF)

215 "Seven members of Yemeni family killed in Saudi-led strike: residents". Reuters. 26 May 2015.

216 "Yemen: 'nowhere safe for civilians': airstrikes and ground attacks in yemen". Retrieved 14 October 2015.

217 Mohammed Ghobari (27 May 2015). "Air strikes kill at least 80 in deadliest bombings of Yemen war". Reuters.

"Nearly 100 people killed in Saudi-led aerial assault on Yemen". Los Angeles Times. 27 May 2015.

218 Yemen's Houthis agree to talks as bombing reportedly kills 58 people". Reuters. 5 June 2015. Retrieved 13 July 2015.

219 Scud missile fired at Saudi Arabia as 38 Yemenis reported killed". Reuters. 7 June 2015. Retrieved 13 July 2015.

5				
2015	7 June[220]	Sanaa	44 people	Local sources
2015	12 June[221]	Old City of Sanaa	6 people	Local sources
2015	13 June[222]	Bait Me'yad, Sanaa	9 people	Medical sources
2015	16 June[223]	Taiz	5 civilians	Amnesty International
2015	19 June[224]	Across Yemen	10 civilians	Local sources
2015	21 June[225]	Across Yemen	15 people	BBC
2015	30 June[226]	Saada	2 people	Local sources

220 Saudi-led air strikes kill 44 in attack on Yemeni army HQ – agency". *Reuters*. 7 June 2015. Retrieved 13 July 2015.

221 "At least six killed as Saudi-led air strikes hit ancient Sanaa: agency". *Reuters*. 12 June 2015. Retrieved 13 July 2015.

222 *"Nine dead in air raid on area inhabited by Yemeni ex-leader's relatives"*. *Reuters*. *13 June 2015. Retrieved 13 July 2015.*

223 *"Yemen: 'nowhere safe for civilians': airstrikes and ground attacks in yemen"*. *Retrieved 14 October 2015.*

224 *"Heavy airstrikes across Yemen; 10 civilians killed"*. *Business Standard*. *Retrieved 13 July 2015.*

225 "مقتل 15 شخصا" في غارات جوية للتحالف في اليمن" – BBC Arabic". Retrieved 9 October 2015.

226 Seven members of Yemeni family killed in Saudi-led strike: residents". *Reuters*. 26 May 2015.

2015	30 June[227]	Taiz	4 civilians	Amnesty International
2015	2 July[228]	Sanaa	8 people	Houthi-controlled Saba News Agency.
2015	3 July[229]	Across Yemen	16 people	Local sources
2015	6 July[230]	Across Yemen	100 people	Local and Medical sources
2015	7 July[231]	Taiz	11 Lahj	Amnesty International
2015	9 July[232]	Taiz	11 Lahj	Amnesty International
2015	25 July[233]	Mokha, Yemen	120 civilians	Associated Press
2015	17 August[234]	Jibla and Al-Jawf	17 civilians	Local officials

227 "Yemen: 'nowhere safe for civilians': airstrikes and ground attacks in yemen". Retrieved 14 October 2015.

228 Eight dead in new Saudi-led strikes on Yemen's Sanaa: agency". *Reuters*. 2 July 2015. Retrieved 13 July 2015.

229 "Saudi-led air strikes on Yemen cities kill 16: Houthis". *Reuters*. 3 July 2015. Retrieved 13 July 2015.

230 Air strikes kill nearly 100 in Yemen, cast shadow on truce talks". *Reuters*. 6 July 2015. Retrieved 13 July 2015.

231 "Yemen: 'nowhere safe for civilians': airstrikes and ground attacks in yemen". Retrieved 14 October 2015.

232 "Yemen: 'nowhere safe for civilians': airstrikes and ground attacks in yemen". Retrieved 14 October 2015.

233 "News from The Associated Press". Retrieved 29 July 2015.

234 "Civilians bear brunt of air strikes in Yemen". *Reuters*. Retrieved 15 November 2015.

201 5				
201 5	19 August[235]	Sanaa	15 civilians	UN
201 5	21 August[236]	Taiz	65 civilians	Doctors Without Borders
201 5	28 August[237]	Taiz	10 people	Reuters
201 5	30 August[238]	Hajjah and Sanaa	40 civilians	Local sources
201 5	5 September[239]	Sanaa	27 civilians	Reuters
201 5	6 September[240]	Al Jawf Governorate	30 people	Reuters

---

235 "Yemen Is No Place for Men, Women and Children". *HuffPost*. Retrieved 15 November 2015.

236 Rick Gladstone (21 August 2015). "Airstrikes Kill Dozens of Civilians in Yemen, Doctors Without Borders Says". *The New York Times*. Retrieved 25 February 2016.

237 https://ara.reuters.com/article/topNews/idARAKCN0QX1WO20150828

238 "Saudi-led coalition air strike kills 36 Yemeni civilians: residents". *Reuters*. 30 August 2015. Retrieved 15 November 2015.

239 "Yemen: 'nowhere safe for civilians': airstrikes and ground attacks in yemen". Retrieved 14 October 2015. https://ara.reuters.com/article/topNews/idARAKCN0R60F320150906?sp=true

240 https://ara.reuters.com/article/topNews/idARAKCN0R60F320150906?sp=true

Year	Date	Location	Casualties	Source
2015	12 September[241]	Across Yemen	16 civilians	Reuters
2015	14 September[242]	Sanaa, Yemen	10 people	Reuters
2015	20 September[243]	Saada	20 People	Reuters
2015	21 September[244]	Hajjah and Sanaa	50 people	Reuters
2015	27 September[245]	Hajjah	30 civilians	Local sources
2015	28 September[246]	Al-Wahijah, Taiz	131 civilians	Medics
2015	8 October[247]	Dhamar, Yemen	25–50 people	Reuters

241 "مسعفون: مقتل 16 مدنيا على الأقل في غارات للتحالف باليمن". Retrieved 9 October 2015.

242 Ten killed in air strike on Sanaa as fighting starts in central Yemen". Retrieved 14 September 2015.

243 "مصادر: مقتل 50 على الأقل باليمن في ضربات جوية نفذها التحالف". Retrieved 9 October 2015.

244 https://ara.reuters.com/article/topNews/idARAKCN0RL1SG20150921?sp=true *Retrieved 9 October 2015.*

245 "Death toll from air strike on Yemen wedding party rises above 130 -medics". *Reuters*. 29 September 2015. Retrieved 5 November 2019.

246 "Death toll from air strike on Yemen wedding party rises above 130 -medics". *Reuters*. 29 September 2015. Retrieved 5 November 2019.

247 "سكان: مقتل 25 يمنيا بينهم ثلاثة عرسان إثر سقوط صاروخ على حفل زفاف" [Residents: 25 people were killed, including three weddings in a rocket strike in Yemen]. *Reuters* (in Arabic). Retrieved 8 October 2015.

201 6	10 January[248]	Saada, Yemen	6 civilians	Doctors Without Borders
201 6	13 January[249]	Bilad al-Rus	15 civilians	Local sources
201 6	27 February[250]	Sanaa	40 civilians	Reuters
201 6	15 March[251]	Mastaba	at least 119 people	UN
201 6	20 June[252]	Sanaa	8 civilians	Yemeni Officials
201 6	7 August[253]	Nehm district	18 civilians	Local officials
201 6	9 August[254]	Sanaa	13 civilians	Reuters
201	13 August[255]	Saada	19 civilians	MSF

248 "MSF-supported hospital bombed in Yemen: death toll rises to six". Médecins Sans Frontières. 17 January 2016

249 Editorial (13 January 2016). "Fifteen Yemeni civilians killed in Saudi-led air strike - residents". Reuters.

250 Khaled Abdullah (27 February 2016). "Arab coalition air strikes kill 40 northeast of Yemen capital – residents". Reuters.

251 Maggie Michael; Jon Gambrell (7 April 2016). "Saudi coalition used US bombs in obliterating Yemen market". The Washington Post.

252 The Associated Press (21 June 2016). "Yemeni Officials Say Coalition Airstrike Kills 8 Civilians". The New York Times. Retrieved 25 June 2016.

253 Almosawa, Shuaib; Nordland, Rod (8 August 2016). "As Peace Talks in Yemen Crumble, Civilians End Up in Cross Hairs Again". The New York Times. Retrieved 13 August 2016.

254 Saudi-led attacks on Yemeni capital resume, 13 killed, residents say". Reuters. 9 August 2016. Retrieved 13 August 2016.

6				
201 6	15 August[256]	Hajjah province	19 civilians	MSF
201 6	10 September[257]	Arhab district	30 people	UN
201 6	21 September[258]	Al Hudaydah Governorate	26 civilians	Reuters
201 6	8 October[259]	Sanaa	140 people	UN
201 6	29 October[260]	Al Hudaydah	60 inmates	Reuters
201 6	28 November[261]	Al Hudaydah	at least 13 civilians	Yemeni officials
201	1 January[262]	Sirwah District	5 civilians	Military officials

255 Almosawa, Shuaib; Nordland, Rod (13 August 2016). "Saudi Coalition Airstrikes in Yemen Kill at Least 19, Mostly Children". *The New York Times*. Retrieved 16 August 2016.

256 *Almosawa, Shuaib; Nordland, Rod (15 August 2016). "Bombing of Doctors Without Borders Hospital in Yemen Kills at Least 15". The New York Times. Retrieved 16 August 2016.*

257 "Yemen conflict: UN disturbed by deadly air strikes on water well". BBC News. 12 September 2016

258 "Yemen: 26 killed by coalition air strike in Hodeidah". Al Jazeera. 22 September 2016

259 "Britain must end all arms exports with Saudi Arabia immediately, campaigners demand". *The Independent*. 10 October 2016.

260 "Saudi-led raid kills 60 at Yemen security site, prison, official says". *Reuters*. 31 October 2016 – via www.reuters.com

261 "Saudi-led airstrike kills at least 13 civilians in Yemen". *Associated Press*. 28 November 2016

262 "Yemen: Bombing, air strike kill nine civilians". Middle East Eye. Retrieved 2 January 2017.

7				
201 7	7 January[263]	Sana'a	12 civilians	Medics
201 7	10 January[264]	Nehm district	8 children	Rescuers
201 7	15 February[265]	north of Sanaa	10 women and children	Reuters
201 7	10 March[266]	Al Khawkhah district	18 civilians	UN
201 7	15 March[267]	Mastaba	119 people	Human Rights Watch
201 7	16 March[268]	Bab-el-Mandeb	42 Somali refugees	UN
201 7	3 April[269]	Sarawah District	8 civilians	Security and tribal officials

263 "8 students killed in Saudi-led airstrikes near Yemen's capital". Xinhua News Agency. 10 January 2017.

264 "8 students killed in Saudi-led airstrikes near Yemen's capital". Xinhua News Agency. 10 January 2017.

265 "Saudi air strike kills 10 women and children in Yemen". The Independent. 17 February 2017.

266 Over 100 civilians killed in a month, including fishermen, refugees, as Yemen conflict reaches two-year mark". The Office of the United Nations High Commissioner for Human Rights (OHCHR). 24 March 2017.

267 "Saudi coalition used U.S. bomb in Yemen market strike that killed 119: report". CBC News.

268 "Saudi-led coalition blamed after helicopter gunship massacres Somali refugees". The Independent. 18 March 2017.

269 "Suspected Saudi-led airstrikes kill 8 in Yemen". Fox News Channel. Retrieved 3 April 2017

2017	17 May[270]	Mawza District	23 civilians	Houthis
2017	17 June[271]	Saada Governorate	24 civilians	Health officials
2017	18 July[272]	al-Atera village, Mawza District	20+ civilians	UN
2017	23 August[273]	Arhab, Sana'a	48+ civilians	Medical officials
2017	26 December[274]	Taiz, Hodeidah	68 civilians	UN
2018	3 April[275]	Hodeidah	14+ civilians	Medics
2018	23 April[276]	Hajja	40+ civilians	Medical officials

270 Suspected Saudi-led raid kills 23 Yemen civilians: rebels". *Gulf Times*. Retrieved 17 May 2017.

271 "24 killed in bombing of Yemen market". *Yahoo News*. Retrieved 18 June 2017.

272 Saudi-led air strikes kill at least 20 Yemeni civilians". CBC News. Retrieved 19 July 2017.

273 *"Air raid in Yemen kills at least 35 people"*. Al Jazeera. Retrieved 23 August 2017.

"Airstrike in Yemen kills dozens at hotel". CNN. Retrieved 24 August 2017.

274 "Yemen civil war: Saudi-led air strikes kill 68 civilians in one day, says UN". *The Independent*. 28 December 2017.

275 "Yemen: Children among 14 dead in Saudi-led air strike on Hodeidah". *Al-Jazeera*. 3 April 2018

276 Yemen war: Saudi-led air strike on wedding 'kills 20'". *BBC News*. 23 April 2018.

201 8	9 August[277]	Saada	51 killed including 40 children	International Committee of the Red Cross; Houthi Health Ministry
201 8	13 October[278]	Al Hudaydah	17 people	Deutsche Welle
201 8	24 October[279]	Al Hudaydah Governorate	21+ civilians	UN
201 9	29 July[280]	Saada Governorate	13+ civilians	Medics
201 9	1 September[281]	Dhamar	100+ civilians	Red Cross (ICRC)
202 0	15 February[282]	Al Jawf Governorate	31+ civilians	UN

---

277 "Yemen war: Saudi-led air strike on bus kills 29 children". *BBC News*. 9 August 2018.

"Yemen buries children killed by air strike, Riyadh insists raid 'legitimate'". *Reuters*. 13 August 2018.

278 "Saudi-led airstrike hits civilians at Yemen market". *Deutsche Welle*. 25 October 2018.

279 Yemen medics say 13 civilians killed in Saudi strike". *France 24*. 29 July 2019.

280 "Saudi-led airstrike hits civilians at Yemen market". *Deutsche Welle*. 25 October 2018.

281 *"Yemen war: More than 100 dead in Saudi-led strike, says Red Cross"*. *BBC News*. 1 September 2019.

282 *"Dozens of Yemeni civilians killed in air strikes after Saudi jet crash"*. *France 24*. 15 February 2020.

A Houthi spokesman stated on 28 April 2015 that the airstrikes had killed 200 members of all pro-Houthi forces since the campaign started.[283] In addition, UNICEF reported on 24 April 2015 that the strikes had killed 64 children[284]

Between 26 March and 21 April, *The New York Times* confirmed 18 airstrikes that resulted in civilian casualties.[285]

According to the United Nations, between 26 March and 10 May 2015, the conflict, killed at least 828 Yemeni civilians, including 91 women and 182 children. One hundred and eighty-two were killed between 4 and 10 May alone, with most of those due to the airstrikes.[286]

On 6 May HRW reported that an airstrike struck a residential home in Saada, killing 27 members of one family, including 17 children[287]and on 26 May, 7 more members of the same family were killed in another airstrike[288]

On 27 May nearly 100 people were killed due to airstrikes hitting Sanaa, Sa'da and Hodeida in the largest ever one-day death toll throughout the conflict.[289]

On 28 June a coalition airstrike hit and damaged the UN compound in Aden, severely damaging the UNDP building and injuring a guard.[290]

On 30 June HRW released a report stating that coalition airstrikes on the northern Yemeni city of Saada, a Houthi rebel stronghold, had killed dozens of civilians and wrecked homes and markets. The group said it had documented a dozen airstrikes on Saada that destroyed or damaged civilian homes, five markets, a school and a petrol station although there was no evidence of military use. "Saada City's streets are littered with bomb craters, destroyed buildings, and other evidence of coalition airstrikes," HRW's Sarah Leah Whitson said in the report[291] and later added. "These attacks appear to be serious laws-of-war violations that need to be properly investigated."[292]

283 *"20 dead as rebels advance in heart of Yemen's Aden"*. *GlobalPost*. *Archived* from the original on 4 July 2015.

284 *"Hundreds of children killed or maimed in deadly month-long fighting in Yemen – UNICEF"*. *UNICEF*. 24 April 2015.

285 "Saudi-Backed Forces Gain Momentum". *The New York Times*. 26 March 2015.

286 "UN preparing vast aid operation in Yemen". *The Peninsula*.

287 Dispatches: Renewed Fighting in Yemen Should Not Mean Renewed Violations". Human Rights Watch. 18 May 2015.

288 "Seven members of Yemeni family killed in Saudi-led strike: residents". *Reuters*. 26 May 2015.

289 "Nearly 100 people killed in Saudi-led aerial assault on Yemen". *Los Angeles Times*. 27 May 2015.

290 United Nations Web Services Section. "United Nations Secretary-General Ban Ki-moon's Statements". Retrieved 13 July 2015.

291 "Rights group says Arab bombings killed dozens of Yemeni civilians". *Reuters*. 30 June 2015. Retrieved 13 July 2015.

292 "Yemen: Unlawful Airstrikes Kill Dozens of Civilians". Human Rights Watch. 13 July 2015. Retrieved 13 July 2015.

On 6 July airstrikes killed over 100 people including more than 30 civilians in Al Joob, Amran.[293] The state-run news agency said that 40 had been killed in a raid on a livestock market in al-Foyoush. Local residents also reported 30 deaths in a raid they said apparently targeted a Houthi checkpoint on the main road between Aden and Lahj. They said 10 of the dead were Houthi fighters. MSF head of mission in Yemen said "It is unacceptable that airstrikes take place in highly concentrated civilian areas where people are gathering and going about their daily lives, especially at a time such as Ramadan."[294]

On 25 July airstrikes killed over 120 civilians in the town of Mokha, marking the deadliest strike yet against civilians. The airstrikes hit workers' housing for a power plant in Mokha, flattening some of the buildings, the officials said. A fire erupted in the area, charring many of the corpses. "It just shows what is the trend now of the airstrikes from the coalition," said Hassan Boucenine of the Geneva-based Doctors Without Borders. "Now, it's a house, it's a market, it's anything." He added that many of the workers had families visiting for the Eid al-Fitr holiday at the end of the holy month of Ramadan. Mokha, populated largely by fisherman, had a reputation as one of the safest places in the country embroiled in war, said Boucenine.[295]

On 18 August AI reported that it had confirmed 141 civilian deaths from eight airstrikes.[296]

On 15 March 2016 Saudi-led airstrikes on a market in Mastaba killed at least 119 people, including 25 children[297]

The attack on 8 October 2016 killed 140 people and injuring 500 persons in one of the single worst death tolls in the two-year war. The United Kingdom is under pressure for exporting arms to Saudi Arabia[298]

Forces working for the internationally recognized government of Yemen claimed of being hit by airstrikes on 29 August 2019, while traveling towards the southern city of Aden. According to a government commander, the airstrike killed around 30 troops. No confirmation has been made on who carried out the attack, however, the commander claimed that a coalition led by Saudi Arabia and the United Arab Emirates is the only warring side in Yemen's 4-year-old conflict that is equipped with airpower.[299]

Civilian airstrike casualties
Airstrikes on hospitals in Yemen

293

294 *"Air strikes kill nearly 100 in Yemen, cast shadow on truce talks". Reuters. 6 July 2015. Retrieved 13 July 2015.*

295 "News from The Associated Press". Retrieved 29 July 2015.

296 *"Amnesty: All sides in Yemen may be guilty of war crimes". Today's Zaman. 18 August 2015. Archived from the original on 26 February 2016*

297 "Saudi coalition massacred 119 Yemenis at market with U.S.-supplied bombs". Salon. 7 April 2016.

298 "Forty Somali refugees killed by Saudi-led bombing campaign in Yemen". Goobjoog. 28 April 2015. Retrieved 28 April 2015.

299 "Yemeni troops hit by airstrikes amid fierce fighting for control of Aden". The Guardian. Retrieved 29 August 2019.

On 24 August 2015, the UN special representative of the secretary-general for children and armed conflict said, that of 402 children killed in Yemen since late March 2015, 73 percent were victims of Saudi coalition-led airstrikes.[300] The UN also said at this time that an average of 30 people had been killed in Yemen every single day since the beginning of the war. On top of this, more than 23,000 had been wounded.[301]

On 11 September, UN Human Rights Commissioner said that of 1,527 civilians killed between 26 March and 30 June, at least 941 people were killed by airstrikes carried out by the Saudi-led coalition.[302]

On 27 October, the OHCHR said that out of 2,615 civilians killed between 26 March and 26 October 2015, 1,641 civilians had reportedly been killed due to airstrikes carried out by the Saudi-led coalition.[303]

The January 2016 report of a UN panel of experts, presented to the UN security council, attributed 60 percent (2,682) of all civilian deaths and injuries in the war since 26 March 2015 to air-launched explosive weapons.[304]

---

300 *"Statement on the situation in Yemen by Leila Zerrougui, Special Representative of the Secretary-General for Children and Armed Conflict"*. UN Office of the SRSG for Children and Armed Conflict. 24 August 2015. *Archived* from the original on 25 August 2015.

D'Almeida, Kanya (25 August 2015). *"Majority of Child Casualties in Yemen Caused by Saudi-Led Airstrikes"*. *Inter Press Service*. *Archived* from the original on 26 August 2015.

301 Ben Norton (24 August 2015). *"4,500 killed in Yemen in 150 Days of Saudi-led bombing"*. *Mondoweiss*.

302 *"Situation of human rights in Yemen – Report of the Office of the United Nations High Commissioner for Human Rights (A/HRC/30/31) – Advance Edited Version"*. UN Human Rights Council. 7 September 2015. *Archived*from the original on 14 September 2015.. PDF: *"Situation of human rights in Yemen – Report of the Office of the United Nations High Commissioner for Human Rights (A/HRC/30/31) – Advance Edited Version"* (PDF). UN Human Rights Council. 7 September 2015. *Archived* from the original on 14 September 2015.

Fitch, Asa; al-Kibsi, Mohammed (10 December 2015). *"Heavy Toll in Yemen Conflict Draws Scrutiny – Civilians bear brunt of damage in war between Saudi-led coalition and Houthi rebels"*. *The Wall Street Journal*. *Archived*from the original on 27 December 2015.

Fahim, Kareem (12 September 2015). *"Airstrikes Take Toll on Civilians in Yemen War"*. *The New York Times*. *Archived* from the original on 13 November 2015.

Kouddous, Sharif Abdel (30 November 2015). *"With US help, Saudi Arabia is obliterating Yemen"*. *GlobalPost*. *Archived* from the original on 22 December 2015.

303 *Regular Press Briefing by the Information Service"*. *UNOG*. 27 October 2015. Archived from *the original* on 29 October 2015.

"UN: Yemen's seven-month violence kills 2,615 civilians". *Anadolu Agency*. 27 October 2015. *Archived* from the original on 30 October 2015.

304 *"Report: Saudi Arabia used U.S.-supplied cluster bombs in Yemen"*. CNN. 3 May 2015. Retrieved 4 May 2015.

On 1 February 2016 Reuters reported: "Mortars and rockets fired at Saudi Arabian towns and villages have killed 375 civilians, including 63 children, since the start of the Saudi-led military campaign in Yemen in late March, Riyadh said."[305]

On 16 September 2016, *The Guardian* reported: "The independent and non-partisan survey, based on open-source data, including research on the ground, records more than 8,600 air attacks between March 2015, when the Saudi-led campaign began, and the end of August this year. Of these, 3,577 were listed as having hit military sites and 3,158 struck non-military sites.... The UN has put the death toll of the 18-month war at more than 10,000, with 3,799 of them being civilians."[306]

In October 2016, a densely populated funeral in Yemen was struck, leaving at least 155 dead[307]and 525 wounded,[308] including the senior military and security officials of the Shia Houthi and loyalists of former president Ali Abdullah Saleh.[309] The attack was reportedly carried out by Saudi Arabia.[310] Saudi Arabia accepts the finding of the Joint Incidents Assessment Team, a setup of coalition states to investigate complaints against coalitions' conduct in Decisive Storm, that coalition's bombardment at a funeral ceremony in Sana'a, in which over 140 people were killed and more than 600 injured, was based on wrong information.[311] Reportedly, the United States is reviewing its policy of support for the Saudi-led coalition. US Secretary of State John Kerry sought assurances from Saudi Arabia that incidents such as the airstrike on a civilian funeral in Sana'a will not happen again. He proposed a cease-fire and a return to talks aiming for a political resolution of the conflict. Deputy Crown Prince Mohammed bin Salman said he hoped to institute a 72-hour cease-fire as soon as possible, provided the Houthis will agree.[312]

In December 2017, Saudis killed and injured 600 Yemenis in 26 days.[313]

---

305 Maclean, William; McDowall, Angus (1 February 2016). "Saudi Arabia says 375 civilians killed on its border in Yemen war". *Reuters*. Archived from the original on 2 February 2016.

306 "One in three Saudi air raids on Yemen hit civilian sites, data shows". *The Guardian*. 16 September 2016.

307 "Yemen: Humanitarian Snapshot – Displacement (as of 31 May 2015)". UN Office for the Coordination of Humanitarian Affairs. 1 June 2015. Archivedfrom the original on 5 June 2015. ("PDF" (PDF). Archived from the original on 5 June 2015.)

308 Khomami, Nadia (8 October 2016). "Airstrikes on Yemen funeral kill at least 140 people, UN official says". *The Guardian*. Retrieved 10 October2016.

309 Khomami, Nadia (8 October 2016). "Airstrikes on Yemen funeral kill at least 140 people, UN official says". *The Guardian*. Retrieved 10 October2016.

310 dam, Withnall (10 October 2016). "Britain and US pile pressure on Saudi Arabia over Yemen funeral bombing". *The Independent*. Retrieved 10 October 2016.

311 JIAT: Yemen funeral targeted based on wrong information; Coalition accepts findings". *Arab News*. 15 October 2016. Retrieved 16 October 2016.

312 Mohammad al Kibsi, Ahmed al Omran, Karen Leigh and Felicia Schwartz, "Yemen raid spurs U.S. review of support", The Wall Street Journal (10 October 2016), p. A13.

313 Saudi's kill and injure 600 Yemeni's in just 26 days - AWDnews". *www.awdnews.com*. Retrieved 20 July 2018.

On 9 August 2018, a school bus was hit by a Saudi airstrike, killing 51 people and injuring 79. 40 of the dead and 56 of the injured were children between the ages of 6 and 11.[314]

In the past few days from 7 November, more than 100 Saudi airstrikes had attacked civilian neighborhoods and a malnutrition clinic run by Save the Children in Hodeidah.[315]

According to the Yemen Data Project, the Saudi-led bombing campaign has killed or injured an estimated 17,729 civilians as of March 2019.[316]

As per the Armed Conflict Location and Event Data Project the Saudi-led coalition has caused around 4,800 civilian deaths and the Houthis have caused around 1,300 out of 7,000 civilian fatalities since 2016. On 16 May 2019, another airstrike in a crowded residential area of Sana'a killed five civilians and injured 31.[317]

List of journalists killed in Yemen

In 2015 Yemen was ranked 168th out of 180 countries in the Reporters Without Borders (RSF) Press Freedom Index. According to an annual round-up published on 29 December 2015 by RSF, six journalists in Yemen (out of 67 worldwide) were killed in 2015 because of their work or while reporting.[318] According to the Committee to Protect Journalists, the Saudi-led coalition between March 2015 and the end of January 2016 killed at least six journalists in airstrikes.[319]

---

314 *Nima Elbagir; Salma Abdelaziz; Sheena McKenzie; Waffa Munayyer. "The schoolboys in Yemen were chatting and laughing. Then came the airstrike".*

315 McKernan, Bethan. "Battle rages in Yemen's vital port as showdown looms". *theguardian.* Retrieved 7 November 2018.

316 *"Study: 17,729 Yemeni Civilians Killed or Injured by U.S.-Backed Strikes". Democracy Now!. 27 March 2019. Retrieved 31 March 2019.*

Raghavan, Sudarsan (27 March 2019). "Airstrike by Saudi-led coalition said to hit near Yemeni hospital, killing 8, including 5 children". The Washington Post. Retrieved 31 March 2019.

317 "Saudi Warplanes, Most Made in America, Still Bomb Civilians in Yemen". *The New York times.* Retrieved 22 May 2019.

318 *"RSF Annual Round-up: 110 journalists killed in 2015". Reporters sans Frontières. 29 December 2015. Archived from the original on 3 January 2016.. PDF: "RSF Annual Round-up: 110 journalists killed in 2015" (PDF). Reporters sans Frontières. 29 December 2015. Archived from the original on 3 January 2016.*

319 *"Freelance journalist killed by Saudi coalition airstrike in Yemen". Committee to Protect Journalists. 19 January 2016. Retrieved 19 January2016.*

"CPJ urges full, independent investigation into killing of journalists in Yemen". Committee to Protect Journalists. 2 February 2016. Retrieved 11 February 2016.

On 17 January 2016, the freelance Yemeni journalist Almigdad Mojalli was killed in an airstrike by the Saudi-led coalition in Jaref, a Houthi-controlled district in the outskirts of Sanaʿa.[320] Mojalli had gone there, working for Voice of America (VOA), to interview survivors of air strikes in Jaref in which up to 21 civilians had been killed days earlier.[321] Rory Peck Trust honored him as "key source of information for visiting journalists" in Yemen.[322] Daniel Martin Varisco, President of the American Institute for Yemeni Studies and Research Professor at Qatar University, said in an obituary that Mojalli's work "was a voice documenting the humanitarian crisis that the world outside Yemen has largely ignored" and a voice that "has been silenced".[323] RSF, CPJ, International Federation of Journalists (IFJ), Yemen Journalists' Syndicate (YJS) and UNESCO condemned Mojalli's death.[324] UNESCO Director-General Irina Bokova and RSF reminded all the parties to the armed conflict in Yemen that they were required to respect and ensure the safety of all journalists by UN Security Council Resolution 2222, adopted in 2015, and by the Geneva Conventions.[325]

---

320 "Airstrike in Yemen Kills Freelance Journalist Working for VOA". Voice of America. 17 January 2016. Archived from the original on 18 January 2016.

[a] "Journalist killed in air strike near Sanaa". Reporters without Borders. 18 January 2016. Archived from the original on 18 January 2016.

321 Journalist killed in air strike near Sanaa". Reporters without Borders. 18 January 2016. Archived from the original on 18 January 2016.

Loveluck, Louisa (17 January 2016). "Leading Yemeni journalist who worked for international media killed in air strike". The Daily Telegraph. Archived from the original on 18 January 2016.

322 "Remembering Almigdad Mojalli – The Yemeni freelancer was killed by airstrikes just outside Sana'a on 17th January". Rory Peck Trust. 19 January 2016. Archived from the original on 21 January 2016.

323 Varisco, Daniel Martin (19 January 2016). "The Voice of which America?". MENA Tidningen. Archived from the original on 21 January 2016.

324 "Journalist killed in air strike near Sanaa". Reporters without Borders. 18 January 2016. Archived from the original on 18 January 2016.

325 "Freelance journalist killed by Saudi coalition airstrike in Yemen". Committee to Protect Journalists. 19 January 2016. Retrieved 19 January2016.
Loveluck, Louisa (19 August 2015). "Yemen 'already looks like Syria after five years of war'". The Daily Telegraph. Retrieved 23 February 2016.

"Yemeni journalist's death in air strike deplored by UNESCO". UN News Service. 20 January 2016. Archived from the original on 21 January 2016.

"Director-General deplores death of journalist Almigdad Mojalli in Yemen". UNESCO. 19 January 2016. Archived from the original on 21 January 2016.

On 21 January 2016, the 17-year-old TV cameraman Hashem al-Hamran was mortally injured by an air-strike by the Saudi-led coalition in the city of Dahian (Saada Governorate), when he was filming bombing raids for the Houthi-run television channel al-Masirah TV. He died from his wounds on 22 January 2016.[326] The YJS, the IFJ and Irina Bokova, Director General of UNESCO, condemned the killing of Hashem Al Hamran.[327]

The director of Yemen TV, Munir al-Hakami, and his wife, Suaad Hujaira, who also worked for the state-owned, Houthi-controlled broadcaster, were killed along with their three children by a coalition air strike on 9 February 2016.[328] They were living in a residential area nowhere near a possible military target;[329] the killing of the two media workers was condemned by the head of UNESCO.[330]

Zaid al-Sharabi, an Emirates News Agency journalist, was killed by a Houthi set bomb which was hidden inside a motocycle and placed near a restaurant in Mokha on 29 January 2019. The bomb killed a total of 6 people and wounded another Emirates News Agency journalist, Faisal Al Thubhani.[331]

2016–20 Yemen cholera outbreak

326 "Further media violations in Yemen: another journalist dead and a newspaper silenced". International Federation of Journalists (IFJ). 27 January 2016. Archived from the original on 10 February 2016.
"CPJ urges full, independent investigation into killing of journalists in Yemen". Committee to Protect Journalists. 2 February 2016. Retrieved 11 February 2016.

327 *"Further media violations in Yemen: another journalist dead and a newspaper silenced". International Federation of Journalists (IFJ). 27 January 2016. Archived from the original on 10 February 2016.*

"Director-General condemns killing of media worker Hashem Al Hamran in Yemen". UN Educational, Scientific and Cultural Organization. 9 February 2016. Archived from the original on 10 February 2016.

328 *Oppenheim, Maya (12 February 2016). "Yemeni journalists and their three children killed in Saudi-led airstrikes in the capital of Yemen". The Independent. Archived from the original on 23 February 2016.*

"Director-General condemns killing of media workers Munir al-Hakimi and Suad Hujaira in Yemen". UN Educational, Scientific and Cultural Organization. Archived from the original on 23 February 2016.

Almosawa, Shuaib (10 February 2016). "Yemen: Airstrike Kills Family in Capital". The New York Times. Archived from the original on 23 February 2016.

329 *Almosawa, Shuaib (10 February 2016). "Yemen: Airstrike Kills Family in Capital". The New York Times. Archived from the original on 23 February 2016.*

330 Director-General condemns killing of media workers Munir al-Hakimi and Suad Hujaira in Yemen". UN Educational, Scientific and Cultural Organization. Archived from the original on 23 February 2016.

331 Reynolds, Ryan (29 January 2019). "Abu Dhabi TV cameraman killed in Yemen market bombing". The National.

In February 2016, the UN Security Council noted that in terms of "numbers of people in need" the humanitarian crisis in Yemen was "the largest in the world"[332] In August 2015, the head of the International Red Cross said, "Yemen after five months looks like Syria after five years."[333]

The U.N. human rights office reported more than 8,100 civilians were killed or wounded between 26 March and the end of 2015, the vast majority from airstrikes by Saudi-led coalition forces.[334]

At the beginning of May 2015, the Office of the UN High Commissioner for Human Rights (OHCHR) said, that there had been "severe destruction of civilian infrastructure, including houses, in many districts" since 26 March.[335] Severe damage caused by attacks on Yemen's essential civilian infrastructure such as airports in Sana'a and Hodeida by the Saudi-led military coalition was obstructing the delivery of much-needed humanitarian assistance and movement of humanitarian personnel according to the International Committee of the Red Cross (ICRC) and Médecins Sans Frontières (MSF).[336]

In the first weeks since 26 March massive destruction of civilian infrastructure particularly happened in Aden and Sa'da, according to OHCHR.[337]

332 _"Security Council Press Statement on Situation in Yemen"_. _UN Security Council_. 18 February 2016. Archived from the original on 20 February 2016.(_"PDF"_. Archived from the original on 20 February 2016.)

333 Loveluck, Louisa (19 August 2015). "Yemen 'already looks like Syria after five years of war'". _The Daily Telegraph_. Retrieved 23 February 2016.

334 Schlein, Lisa (5 January 2016). "Yemen War Taking Big Toll on Civilians". Voice of America. Archived from the original on 11 January 2016.

335 "Press briefing notes on Yemen, Serbia, Honduras and Albinism website launch". Office of the High Commissioner for Human Rights. Archived from the original on 5 May 2015. Retrieved 7 May 2015.

336 _"Yemen: MSF and ICRC alarmed by attacks on country's infrastructure and humanitarian lifelines"_. _Médecins Sans Frontières (MSF)_. 4 May 2015. Archived from the original on 16 February 2016.

"Yemen: UN relief official urges 'safe and reliable' access to Sana'a airport to deliver critical aid". _UN News Centre_. 4 May 2015. Archived from the original on 16 February 2016.

"Statement by the Humanitarian Coordinator for Yemen, Johannes Van Der Klaauw (4 May 2015)". _UN Office for the Coordination of Humanitarian Affairs, UN Humanitarian Coordinator in Yemen_. 4 May 2015. Archived from the original on 16 February 2016. (_"PDF"_ (PDF). Archived from the original on 16 February 2016.

337 _Press briefing notes on Hungary, Yemen and Saudi Arabia"_. _UN Office of the High Commissioner for Human Rights_. 22 May 2015. Archived from the original on 23 May 2015.

"Yemen: UN rights office urges all parties to adhere to international law as civilian toll grows". _UN News Centre_. 22 May 2015. Archived from the original on 16 February 2016.

In August 2015, air attacks of the Saudi-led coalition on port facilities at Al-Hudaydah "in clear contravention of international humanitarian law", said Under-Secretary-General for Humanitarian Affairs and Emergency Relief Coordinator Stephen O'Brien[338]

In mid-February 2016, Stephen O'Brien said the situation in Yemen was a "humanitarian catastrophe", with 21 million people in need of some kind of aid, 7.6 million people "severely food-insecure", and over 3.4 million children out of school.[339] O'Brien noted the situation had not been helped by the diversion of an aid vessel by coalition forces.[340]

According to Lamya Khalidi, an archaeologist: *At least sixty of Yemen's monuments have been damaged or destroyed* in the bombing campaign by Saudi-led coalition in March 2015. Among these monuments are unique archaeological monuments, old cities, museums, mosques, churches and tombs.[341]

Timeline

On 26 March, Interior Ministry officials linked to Ansar Allah documented that 23 civilians had been killed and 24 wounded. Among the dead were 5 children, ages 2 to 13, 6 women and an elderly man. The wounded included 12 children, ages 3 to 8, and 2 women due to airstrike against Sana'a particularly in Bani Hawat, a predominantly Houthi neighborhood near Sanaa's airports and al-Nasr, near the presidential palace. HRW documented the deaths of 11 civilians, including 2 women and 2 children, other than those provided by the Yemeni officials along with 14 more wounded, including 3 children and 1 woman. According to AI, that bombing destroyed at least 14 homes in Bani Hawat.[342]

On 31 March, OCHA reported that 13 of 22 Governorates were affected and highlighted infrastructure effects that detailed coalition bombing of a refugee camp that killed 29 and injured 40. Fuel shortages in the south threatened water access to citizens and in Lahj, electricity and water services had not been functioning for several days.[343] Later that day, AI reported that at least six civilians, including four children, were burned to death as a result of an airstrike. It reported that two fuel stations were destroyed. In al-Kadima area in al-Kita, several passengers were killed in a car that had stopped to refuel and a worker was injured. The third strike, apparently aimed at a passing fuel tanker, set fire to at least three civilian homes. AI then stated that "it is becoming increasingly apparent that the

338 *Yemen Humanitarian Bulletin No 1 – 27 August 2015"*. *UN Office for the Coordination of Humanitarian Affairs. 27 August 2015. Archived from the original on 28 August 2015. ("PDF" (PDF). Archived from the original on 28 August 2015.)*

339 Humanitarian catastrophe' unfolding in Yemen: UN". Al JazeeraEnglish. 17 February 2016. Retrieved 17 February 2016.

340 Humanitarian catastrophe' unfolding in Yemen: UN". Al JazeeraEnglish. 17 February 2016. Retrieved 17 February 2016

341 *Fenton-Harvey, Jonathan. "Yemen suffers cultural vandalism during its war".*

https://www.cambridge.org/core/services/aop-cambridge-core/content/view/53D08264CAACB808618BCF9D70053D25/S0020743817000691a.pdf/div-class-title-the-destruction-of-yemen-and-its-cultural-heritage-div.pdf

342 Yemen: Saudi-led Airstrikes Take Civilian Toll, Says HRW". Eurasia Review. 28 March 2015. Archived from the original on 2 April 2015. Retrieved 30 March 2015.

343 "Yemen: Escalating Conflict Situation Report No. 1 (as of 31 March 2015)". United Nations Office for the Coordination of Humanitarian Affairs.

Saudi Arabian-led coalition is turning a blind eye to civilian deaths and suffering caused by its military intervention."[344]

On 17 April, OCHA reported on the increasing deterioration of the humanitarian situation, reporting airstrikes hitting in Saada City a water tank, the electricity station, a petrol station, a plastics processing factory, a shopping centre and a housing complex. Several days earlier, airstrikes had hit private homes, the post office, a community centre, government offices, markets and vehicles. Local partners estimated about 50 dead within the past week. In Sana'a residential neighborhoods near Assir, Ayban and Faj Attan were affected due to their proximity to military camps. In Amran, airstrikes hit a petrol station, an educational institute and a bridge. According to local reports, a local water corporation in Hajjah (Abbs District) was hit. The report also stated that civilian casualties were under-reported as families without access to hospitals bury their members at home.[345]

On 20 April coalition airstrikes hit the Fajj Atan military base, causing a large explosion that killed 38 civilians and injured over 500. The airstrike also targeted the office of Yemen Today, a TV network owned by Ali Abdullah Saleh, killing three and injuring other workers. An eyewitness reported that emergency rooms were overwhelmed.[346] The head of the ICRC in Yemen later clarified that 90 people had died during this attack.[347]

On 21 April the BBC reported a warning from the UN about worsening health services and a dire need for medicines.[348]

On 24 April UNICEF released a report stating that since the start of the military intervention, 115 children had been killed, with at least 64 from aerial bombardment. The F-14's of Saudi Arabia often strike Militia hold outs that miss and hit shelters the homeless and houses.[349]

According to OCHA's fifth report, released on 26 April, humanitarian operations would come to a complete halt within two weeks and hospitals in both Sanaa and Aden would close completely due to the lack of fuel. The lack of fuel affected water supplies. Markets in affected governorates are not able to provide food, with wheat grain and flour prices rising by 42% and 44%, respectively. The healthcare system faced an imminent collapse with hospitals struggling to operate due to lack of medicines and supplies. Essential medicine prices increased by 300%.

---

344 "Yemen: At least six civilians burn to death in further airstrikes overnight". Amnesty International.

345 "Yemen: Escalating Conflict Situation Report No. 4" (PDF). United Nations Office for the Coordination of Humanitarian Affairs. 17 April 2015.

346 Yemen violence kills 944, injures 3,487; WHO". 21 April 2015. Retrieved 26 April 2015.

Air strike on missile base in Yemen capital kills 25, wounds hundreds". Reuters. 20 April 2015. Retrieved 26 April 2015.

347 Life under siege in Yemen: 'Bullets and shrapnel came into the house'". The Guardian.

348 "Yemen conflict: Dozens killed in Saudi-led air strikes". BBC News. 21 April 2015. Retrieved 21 April 2015.

349 Hundreds of children killed or maimed in deadly month-long fighting in Yemen – UNICEF". UNICEF. 24 April 2015.

Casualties from 19 March to 22 April reached 1,080 (28 children and 48 women) and 4,352 wounded (80 children and 143 women). According to the WFP, 12 million people were food insecure, a 13% rise.[350]

On 29 April OCHA reported that airstrikes hit SIA on 28 April, damaging the runway and hampering aid deliveries. Airstrikes were also reported at Al Hudayda Airport and Saada. Widespread internet and phone disruptions were reported in several governorates due to the lack of fuel and electricity. On 25 April, the Yemen Public Telecommunications Corporation warned that unless the fuel crisis was resolved, telecommunication services (mobile phones, internet, and land lines) would shut down within a week. The disruption in communication was affecting information flow on humanitarian needs and operations. On 29 April, Haradh was heavily bombarded, including areas near the main hospital. Food distribution and aid would reportedly stop within a week if additional fuel could not be obtained. As of 29 April the Al Hudaydah Governorate ran out of fuel and aid operations could not be completed.[351]

On 30 April OCHA's Flash Update 22 reported that airstrikes hit the only main roads that connect the Sana'a Governorate with Ibb. It also indicated that over 3,410 people from Yemen had arrived in Somalia since the fighting escalated, with 2,285 arrivals registered in Puntland and 1,125 registered in the Somaliland. A further 8,900 migrants were registered in Djibouti, 4,700 of whom were third country nationals.[352]

On 4 May coalition airstrikes hit SIA, destroying a cargo ship and other planes used to transport food and supplies.[353] OCHA reported that several airstrikes hit the Al Hudayda airport and surrounding areas in Al Hudayda City. In Aden, the districts of Craiter and Al-Muala were without electricity, water and telecommunication for over a week according to residents[354]

Van der Klaauw emphasized the effects on persons with disabilities stating that over 3,000,000 people with disabilities could not meet their basic needs. The conflict forced more than 300 centres to close. He added that they were especially concerned about an airstrike that targeted a military field hospital.[355]

On 6 May, the OCHA reported lack of fuel to support humanitarian operations beyond one week, with fuel and food prices continuing to increase.[356] The World Food

350 "Yemen: Escalating Conflict Situation Report No. 5" (PDF). United Nations Office for the Coordination of Humanitarian Affairs. 26 April 2015.

351 *Yemen: Escalating Conflict Flash Update 21 – 29 April 2015"*. UN Office for the Coordination of Humanitarian Affairs. 29 April 2015. Archivedfrom the original on 16 May 2015. ("*PDF*" (PDF). Archived from the original on 16 May 2015.)

352 "Yemen: Escalating Conflict Flash Update 22" (PDF). ReliefWeb. 30 April 2015. Retrieved 25 February 2016.

353 "Planes burn at Yemen airport following airstrikes". *The Washington Post*. 4 May 2015. Archived from the original on 5 May 2015.

354 "Yemen: Escalating Conflict Flash Update 24" (PDF). ReliefWeb. Retrieved 10 June 2017.

355 "Yemen conflict death toll nears 650, with UN rights office spotlighting plight of 3 million disabled". UN News Centre. 5 May 2015. Archived from the original on 8 May 2015.

356 *"Yemen: Escalating Conflict Situation Report No. 6"*. United Nations Office for the Coordination of Humanitarian Affairs. 6 May 2015. Archived from the original on 15 May 2015. ("*Yemen: Escalating Conflict Situation Report No. 6*" (PDF). United Nations Office for the Coordination of Humanitarian Affairs. Archived from the original on 15 May 2015.)

Programme declared that shortages of fuel has changed to a serious threat for hospitals and food supplies. Edward Santiago, country director for Save the Children, said in statement a short time ceasefire is not enough to allow for humanitarian supplies.[357]

On 7 May, trade sources stated that merchant ships had been delayed weeks Yemen and in one case, following inspection and approval, a food supply ship was denied access. The food crisis increased to include over 20 million people (80% of the population) going hungry.[358] Airstrikes destroyed a mine factory and a communications center. Local sources reported that 13 villagers were killed due to shelling near the border.[359]

On 18 May, HRW documented airstrikes that hit homes and markets and killed and wounded civilians. HRW documented the bombing of four markets.[360]

On 21 May, OCHA reported airstrikes that hit two farms adjacent to a humanitarian facility in Hajjah Governorate and resulted in civilian casualties. A warehouse containing humanitarian supplies was damaged in another strike. In Sa'adah City, satellite imagery analysis identified widespread damage to infrastructure with 1,171 structures affected, damaged or destroyed. The analysis showed that as of 17 May, 35 impact craters existed within the city, mostly along the runway of Sa'ada airport. Similar imagery of Aden identified 642 affected structures, including 327 destroyed. Local partners reported that 674 schools were forced to close in Sana'a, affecting 551,000 students.[361]

Fuel prices increased by over 500% and food supplies by 80% since 26 March. The continued restrictions on the arrival of goods via air and sea ports, and insecurity on roads, restricted the delivery of essential supplies. In Sana'a, security concerns due to airstrikes prevented delivery of food assistance.

On 21 May, five Ethiopian migrants were killed and two others injured in an airstrike that hit open space 500 metres from an IOM-managed Migrant Response Centre. With continued conflict and import restrictions, Emergency (IPC Phase 4) outcomes were likely in the coming month. In six governorates, reports from OCHA partners show that basic food items are no longer available (Aden, Abyan, Al Dhale'e, Al Bayda, Lahj, Sa'ada).[362]

On 3 June, The Operations Room of the Ministry of Health in Sana'a was damaged. It manages emergency operations nationwide[363]

---

357 "Aid agencies warn fuel shortages may end their work in Yemen". *Reuters*. 6 May 2015. Retrieved 7 May 2015.

358 "Yemen Conflict Delays Food Ships, Backs Up Deliveries". Voice of America. Retrieved 11 May 2015.

359 *Mohammed Ghobari; Mohammed Mukhashaf (8 May 2015). "Saudi-led coalition bombs Houthis in north Yemen, offers five-day truce". Reuters. Retrieved 11 May 2015.*

360 Dozens killed by Saudi bombardments in Sa'ada". Saba News Agency. Retrieved 11 May 2015.

361 *"Yemen: Escalating Conflict Flash Update 35 – 21 May 2015". UN Office for the Coordination of Humanitarian Affairs. 21 May 2015. Archivedfrom the original on 22 May 2015.* (PDF)

362 "Yemen: Escalating Conflict Situation Report No. 8" (PDF). United Nations Office for the Coordination of Humanitarian Affairs. 22 May 2015. Retrieved 25 February 2016.

363 *"Yemen: Deteriorating Humanitarian Crisis Situation Report No. 10 (as of 3 June 2015)". UN Office for the Coordination of Humanitarian Affairs. 5 June 2015. Archived from the original on 6*

On 5 June, *The Washington Post* reported that several Yemeni cultural and heritage strikes had been repeatedly targeted by Saudi airstrikes. Reports stated that Al-Qahira Castle, the 1,200-year-old al-Hadi Mosque and Dhamar Museum with over 12,500 artifacts[364] were destroyed and the Great Dam of Marib was hit.[365]

On 17 June, an OCHA report highlighted that food security had continued to worsen, with 19 out of 22 governorates now classified 'crisis' or 'emergency'. Half the population was 'food insecure' and nearly a quarter 'severely food insecure. A joint analysis of household food security by the UN Food and Agriculture Organization (FAO) WFP and the Ministry of Planning and International Cooperation in Yemen (MoPIC) found that Yemen was sliding into catastrophe. More than six million Yemenis were then in a Phase 4 Emergency, and nearly 6.9 million people are in a Phase 3 Crisis: These figures indicate that Yemen was approaching a complete breakdown in food security and health.[366]

On 26 July, the OCHA announced that airstrikes hit the residential complex of the Al Mukha Power Station in Al Mukha District, Taiz Governorate with health facilities reporting 55 deaths and 96 injuries and media reports as high as 120, all civilians.[367]

On 27 August, the OCHA announced that airstrikes targeting that Al-Hudaydah port facilities late on 17 August and early 18 August had brought the port activities to a near halt and that the port was empty of all vessels and remained non-operational. A UN-chartered aid vessel carrying 2,230 MT of mixed food commodities left the port and was rerouted to Djibouti.[368]

On 5 January 2016, an airstrike by the Saudi-led military coalition hit the Al Noor Center for Care and Rehabilitation of Blind, in the Safiah district of Sana'a,[369] the capital's only

---

June 2015. ("PDF" (PDF). Archived from the original on 6 June 2015.)

364 Yemen: Escalating Conflict Situation Report No. 8" (PDF). United Nations Office for the Coordination of Humanitarian Affairs. 22 May 2015. Retrieved 25 February 2016.

365 *Taylor, Adam (5 June 2015). "The world may be ignoring the destruction of cultural treasures in Yemen". The Washington Post. Retrieved 13 July 2015.*

366 *"Yemen: New Analysis Shows Deepening Food Crisis – Crisis Update 40 – 17 June 2015 (1000hrs)". UN Office for the Coordination of Humanitarian Affairs. 17 June 2015. Archived from the original on 19 June 2015.("PDF" (PDF). Archived from the original on 19 June 2015.)*

367 "Yemen: Taizz airstrikes Crisi Update 42" (PDF). ReliefWeb. 26 July 2015. Retrieved 25 February 2016.

368 *"Yemen Humanitarian Bulletin No 1 – 27 August 2015". UN Office for the Coordination of Humanitarian Affairs. 27 August 2015. Archived from the original on 28 August 2015. ("PDF" (PDF). Archived from the original on 28 August 2015.)*

369 *Oakford, Samuel (5 January 2016). "The Saudi Coalition Bombed A Rehabilitation Center for Blind People in Yemen". Vice News.*

MacDonald, Alex (5 January 2016). "Yemen centre for blind 'hit in Saudi coalition air raid'". Middle East Eye. Archived from the original on 7 January 2016.

"Yemen: Houthis Endangered School for Blind – Coalition Airstrike Shows Added Risks for People With Disabilities". Human Rights Watch. 13 January 2016. Archived from the original on 14 January 2016.

center, school, and home for people with visual disabilities.[370] Five people were injured. Human Rights Watch and media reported, if the bomb had exploded, the damage would have been much worse.[371] Human Rights Watch blamed both the Saudi-led coalition for hitting civilian targets and the Houthi militants battling the coalition. HRW said Houthi militants were partially to blame for using civilian sites for military purposes. Armed Houthis were stationed near the Al Noor center, putting the students at risk.[372]

On 20 April 2016 the UN General Assembly Security Council in a report covering the period January to December 2015 "verified a sixfold increase in the number of children killed and maimed compared with 2014, totalling 1,953 child casualties (785 children killed and 1,168 injured). More than 70 per cent were boys. Of the casualties, 60 per cent (510 deaths and 667 injuries) were attributed to the Saudi Arabia-led coalition."[373]

On 8 October 2016, airstrikes by Saudi-led coalition force kill 140 people and injuring 500 persons in one of the single worst death tolls in the two-year war. There are coalitions between Saudi Arabia and his allies in the subject. Also, the United Kingdom is under pressure for exporting Lucrative Arms and weapons to Saudi Arabia.[374]

---

370 _"Yemen: Houthis Endangered School for Blind – Coalition Airstrike Shows Added Risks for People With Disabilities"_. _Human Rights Watch_. 13 January 2016. _Archived_ from the original on 14 January 2016.

Murdock, Heather; Mojalli, Almigdad (14 January 2016). "Houthis and Saudi Coalition Put Students at Risk, Rights Group Says". Voice of America. Archived from the original on 18 January 2016.

371 _"Yemen: Houthis Endangered School for Blind – Coalition Airstrike Shows Added Risks for People With Disabilities"_. _Human Rights Watch_. 13 January 2016. _Archived_ from the original on 14 January 2016.

Murdock, Heather; Mojalli, Almigdad (14 January 2016). "Houthis and Saudi Coalition Put Students at Risk, Rights Group Says". Voice of America. Archived from the original on 18 January 2016.

Murdock, Heather (14 January 2016). "Rights Group: Houthis, Saudi Coalition Put Blind Students at Risk". Voice of America. Archived from the original on 18 January 2016.

372 _"Yemen: Houthis Endangered School for Blind – Coalition Airstrike Shows Added Risks for People With Disabilities"_. _Human Rights Watch_. 13 January 2016. _Archived_ from the original on 14 January 2016.

Murdock, Heather; Mojalli, Almigdad (14 January 2016). "Houthis and Saudi Coalition Put Students at Risk, Rights Group Says". Voice of America. Archived from the original on 18 January 2016.

Murdock, Heather (14 January 2016). "Rights Group: Houthis, Saudi Coalition Put Blind Students at Risk". Voice of America. Archived from the original on 18 January 2016.

373 https://www.globalsecurity.org/military/library/report/2016/a-70-836.pdf page 27, paragraph 167

374 Gardner, Frank (10 October 2016). _"Yemen conflict: 'Saudi-led coalition plane' hit funeral"_. _BBC News_.

On 2 August 2018, *The New York Times* reported that at least 30 people were killed when the Saudi-led coalition air force hit a fish market, the entrance to the main hospital and a security compound.[375]

On 9 August 2018, a Saudi airstrike in Dahyan hit a school bus causing approximately 51 deaths. Many of these deaths were schoolchildren and other civilians.

On 8 October 2019, Yemen made an agreement to hand over Aden to Saudi Arabia.[376]

On 7 February 2020, Yemeni hospitals were attacked, leaving more than thousands of civilians in need of immediate medical attention followed by a disrupted healthcare facility. The attack was a result of clashes between warring parties of Yemen; Saudi Arabian-led intervention in Yemen and Houthis.[377]

Saada

Saada was the governorate of origin of 500,794 IDPs (out of 2,509,068 in total) as of December 2015.[378]

On 18 April, an airstrike in Saada hit an Oxfam warehouse, damaging humanitarian supplies and killing at least one civilian. Aid groups widely condemned the strike.[379]

On 8 and 9 May 2015, large-scale displacement was reported in Saada to neighbouring areas, after the Saudi-led military coalition declared the entire Saada governorate a "military zone" and started heavy airstrikes.[380] Around 70,000 people, including 28,000 children, fled from the Governorate of Sa'ada. The Save the Children's Country Director in Yemen, Edward Santiago, said that many more were "largely unable to flee for safety because of the de facto blockade imposed by the coalition leading to severe fuel

375 Kalfood, Mohammed Ali; Coker, Margaret (2 August 2018). "Saudis Escalate Siege of Port in Yemen, Alarming Aid Groups". *The New York Times*.

376 "Yemen: Imminent agreement to hand over Aden to Saudi Arabia". *Middle East Monitor*. 8 October 2019.

377 *"Hospitals in Yemen attacked, disrupting healthcare for thousands of vulnerable civilians"*. *UN News*. Retrieved 10 February 2020.

"Attacks on Marib hospitals limit medical services available to thousands of displaced people" (PDF). *Relief Web*. Retrieved 10 February 2020.

378 *Task Force on Population Movement, 6th Report, 10 December 2015"*. *UN Office for the Coordination of Humanitarian Affairs, UN High Commissioner for Refugees, Protection Cluster. 10 December 2015. Archived from the original on 15 December 2015. ("PDF" (PDF). Archived from the original on 15 December 2015.)*

379 "Oxfam Condemns Coalition Bombing of a Warehouse Containing Vital Humanitarian Aid". Oxfam. 20 April 2015.

380 *"2016 Humanitarian Needs Overview"*. *UN Office for the Coordination of Humanitarian Affairs. 22 November 2015. Archived from the original on 24 November 2015 – via ReliefWeb.*; PDF: *"2016 Humanitarian Needs Overview"* (PDF). Archived from the original on 24 November 2015.
"2015 Yemen Humanitarian Needs Overview (Revised)". *UN Office for the Coordination of Humanitarian Affairs. 12 June 2015. Archived from the original on 12 June 2015. ("PDF" (PDF). Archived from the original on 12 June 2015.)*

shortages".[381]On 9 May 2015, the U.N. Humanitarian Coordinator for Yemen, Johannes van der Klaauw, condemned the air strikes on Saada city as being in breach of international humanitarian law[382]

In August 2015 the Agency for Technical Cooperation and Development (ACTED) reported that "the crisis has taken an immeasurably heavy toll on civilians in this poor, rural governorate, causing death, injury and frequent damage and destruction of infrastructure."[383]

In January 2016 the Houthi-controlled Saada area, including medical facilities run by Médecins Sans Frontières (MSF), received almost daily attacks. Michael Seawright, a Saada-based MSF project coordinator, said that they treated a high number of casualties, many with severe injuries. The Shiara hospital in Razeh District in Saada City, the only hospital with a trauma centre in the governorate of Saada and in most of northern Yemen, was hit on 10 January, and several people were killed, including medical personnel. MSF had been working in the facility since November 2015.[384]

Sana'a

457.502 IDPs (out of 2,509,068 in total) originated from Sana'a Governorate and Sana'a city as of December 2015.[385]

After the Old City of Sana'a was heavily bombed in May 2015, causing severe damage to many of its historic buildings, Director-General of UNESCO, Irina Bokova, said "I am

381 Aid Agencies Call For an Immediate and Permanent Cease Fire as an Additional 70,000 People Flee Coalition Airstrikes in Northern Yemen". Save the Children. 10 May 2015. Archived from the original on 11 May 2015. Retrieved 12 May 2015

382 Miles, Tom (9 May 2015). "Saudi-led strikes in Yemen break international law: U.N. coordinator". Reuters U.S. Archived from the original on 10 May 2015.

"Statement by the Humanitarian Coordinator for Yemen, Johannes Van Der Klaauw (9 May 2015)" (PDF). UN Office for the Coordination of Humanitarian Affair, UN Humanitarian Coordinator in Yemen. 9 May 2015. Archived from the original on 10 May 2015.

383 Seawright, Michael (27 January 2016). "Yemen: 'I Have Never Seen Such Destruction'". Médecins Sans Frontières. Archived from the original on 28 January 2016.

384 Seawright, Michael (27 January 2016). "Yemen: 'I Have Never Seen Such Destruction'". Médecins Sans Frontières. Archived from the original on 28 January 2016.

"Yemen: Another MSF-supported hospital bombed – Update – As of 11 January, the death toll has risen to five". Médecins Sans Frontières. 10 January 2016. Archived from the original on 11 January 2016. (Update: 11 January 2016); Cf.: "MSF-Supported Hospital Bombed in Northern Yemen – Update January 11, 2016". Médecins Sans Frontières. 10 January 2016. Archived from the original on 28 January 2016. (Update: 11 January 2016) and "MSF-supported hospital bombed in Yemen: death toll rises to six". Médecins Sans Frontières. 10 January 2016. Archived from the original on 21 January 2016. (Update: 17 January 2016)

385 Task Force on Population Movement, 6th Report, 10 December 2015". UN Office for the Coordination of Humanitarian Affairs, UN High Commissioner for Refugees, Protection Cluster. 10 December 2015. Archived from the original on 15 December 2015. ("PDF" (PDF). Archived from the original on 15 December 2015.)

particularly distressed by the news concerning air strikes on heavily populated areas such as the cities of Sana'a and Saa'dah."[386]

Following a surge in aerial bombing raids in the Old City of Sana'a in June 2015, the UN warned, that the country's extensive archaeological and historic heritage had been increasingly under threat.[387] In July 2015, the Old City of Sana'a, which had sustained serious damage due to armed conflict, was added to List of World Heritage in Danger.[388]

On 6 September 2015, Al Sabaeen paediatric hospital in Sana'a had to be evacuated after a nearby airstrike. The United Nations' Office for the Coordination of Humanitarian Affairs (UN-OCHA) described the event as "a severe blow to a tattered health system". [511] Before its closure the Al Sabaeen paediatric hospital—standing amid bombed out buildings in the center of Sana'a—had been the primary paediatric hospital in the area.[389] "Before the crisis it had a catchment population of about 300,000; but, since the crisis that number has risen to almost 3 million, with the entire governorate reliant on it for specialist care," said Save the Children spokesperson Mark Kaye.[390]

A joint report by the UK-based charity Action on Armed Violence (AOAV) and the UN-OCHA, that concluded that airstrikes were responsible for 60 percent of civilian

386 "UNESCO Director-General calls on all parties to protect Yemen's cultural heritage". UNESCO World Heritage Convention. 12 May 2015. Archivedfrom the original on 21 May 2015.

387 "Yemen: UN reports uptick in civilian deaths as fighting in country continues". UN News Centre. 16 June 2015. Archived from the original on 17 June 2015.

388 "Yemen's Old City of Sana'a and Old Walled City of Shibam added to List of World Heritage in Danger". UNESCO World Heritage Centre. 2 July 2015. Archived from the original on 2 July 2015.

Key Yemen Hospital on the Brink of Closure as Airstrikes Intensify on Sana'a". Save the Children. 30 August 2015. Archived from the original on 31 August 2015.

Ridgwell, Henry (2 September 2015). "Yemen 'on Brink of Disaster' as Medical Shortages Soar". Voice of America. Archived from the original on 9 November 2015. Cf.: Ridgwell, Henry (2 September 2015). "Yemen 'on Brink of Disaster' as Medical Shortages Soar". Voice of America. Archived from the original on 9 November 2015.

389 Key Yemen Hospital on the Brink of Closure as Airstrikes Intensify on Sana'a". Save the Children. 30 August 2015. Archived from the original on 31 August 2015.

Ridgwell, Henry (2 September 2015). "Yemen 'on Brink of Disaster' as Medical Shortages Soar". Voice of America. Archived from the original on 9 November 2015. Cf.: Ridgwell, Henry (2 September 2015). "Yemen 'on Brink of Disaster' as Medical Shortages Soar". Voice of America. Archived from the original on 9 November 2015.

390 "Key Yemen Hospital on the Brink of Closure as Airstrikes Intensify on Sana'a". Save the Children. 30 August 2015. Archived from the original on 31 August 2015.

casualties in the first seven months of 2015,[391] came to the result, that more than half (53 per cent) of the reported civilian toll was recorded in Sana'a and surrounding districts[392]

On 7 January 2016, HRW reported and condemned that the Saudi Arabia-led coalition forces had used cluster bombs on residential areas of Sanaa on 6 January.[393] On 8 January the United Nations warned that their use could be a war crime.[394] The UN Secretary-General Ban Ki-moon said he was "particularly concerned about reports of intense airstrikes in residential areas and on civilian buildings in Sana'a, including the Chamber of Commerce, a wedding hall and a centre for the blind".[395]

HRW-investigation of six apparently unlawful airstrikes in residential areas of Sanaa city in September and October 2015, that (according to HRW) failed to distinguish civilians from military objectives or caused disproportionate civilian loss[396]

391   Craig, Iona (16 November 2015). "The Agony of Saada – U.S. and Saudi Bombs Target Yemen's Ancient Heritage". The Intercept. Archived from the original on 21 November 2015.

Perkins, Robert (22 September 2015). "State of Crisis: Explosive Weapons in Yemen". UN Office for the Coordination of Humanitarian Affairs, Action on Armed Violence. Archived from the original on 28 October 2015. ("PDF"(PDF). Archived from the original on 28 October 2015., "original PDF"(PDF). Archived from the original on 10 November 2015.)

392   "Yemen Humanitarian Bulletin No 3 – 29 September 2015 [EN/AR]". UN Office for the Coordination of Humanitarian Affairs. 29 September 2015. Archived from the original on 10 November 2015. ("PDF" (PDF). Archived from the original on 10 November 2015.)

393   Yemen: Coalition Drops Cluster Bombs in Capital – Indiscriminate Weapon Used in Residential Areas". Human Rights Watch. 7 January 2016. Archived from the original on 7 January 2016.

394   "UN chief 'deeply concerned' about intensification of airstrikes and ground fighting in Yemen". UN News Service. 8 January 2016. Archived from the original on 9 January 2016.

"Statement attributable to the Spokesman for the Secretary-General on Yemen". United Nations. 8 January 2016. Archived from the original on 9 January 2016.

395   "Statement attributable to the Spokesman for the Secretary-General on Yemen". United Nations. 8 January 2016. Archived from the original on 9 January 2016.

"UN warns cluster bomb use in Yemen may amount to war crime". Business Standard. AFP. 9 January 2016. Retrieved 21 December 2015.

Date	Location	Objectives struck	Civilians killed (at least)				Civilians injured (if known)
			men	women	children	total	
4 September	Hadda Neighborhood, San a'a	four-story apartment building	0	1	2	3	
18 September	Marib Street, Sana'a	house and unused iron lathe workshop	3	1	1	5	8
18 September	Old City, Sana'a	buildings of the World Heritage Site	4	2	7	13	12
21 September	Al-Hassaba Neighborhood, San a'a	homes in the densely populated residential area	3	6	11	20	?
23 September	Al-Asbahi Neighborhood, San a'a	buildings in the residential neighborho od	7	2	10	19	?
26 October	Thabwa, Sana'a	buildings in the residential neighborho od					2
civilian airstrike casualties for all 6 airstrikes, investigated by HRW (report of 21 December 2015)			60				?

396 "Yemen: Coalition Bombs Homes in Capital – Saudi-led Forces, US Fail to Investigate Alleged Unlawful Attacks". Human Rights Watch. 21 December 2015. Archived from the original on 21 December 2015.

Internally Displaced Persons (IDP)

In April and May 2015 mass displacement was observed primarily in Saada, Amran and Hajjah governorates as airstrikes and shelling intensified in the north of Yemen.[397]

On 13 April, OCHA reported that (as of 11 April) more than 120,000 people were estimated to have been internally displaced since 26 March 2015.[398]

On 17 May the UN, citing Yemen's health services, said that as of 15 May 545,000 had been internally displaced because of the war,[399] up from 450,000 announced on 15 May 2015.[400]

On 1 June, the UN announced that 1,019,762 people had been internally displaced as of 28 May 2015.[401]

On 6 July the UN announced that as of 2 July there were 1,267,590 internally displaced people in Yemen.[402]

---

397 *2015 Yemen Humanitarian Needs Overview (Revised)"*. *UN Office for the Coordination of Humanitarian Affairs. 12 June 2015. Archived from the original on 12 June 2015. ("PDF" (PDF). Archived from the original on 12 June 2015.)*

398

399 *"Yemen: Humanitarian Pause, Situation Report No. 4"*. *UN Office for the Coordination of Humanitarian Affairs. 17 May 2015. Archived from the original on 18 May 2015. ("PDF" (PDF). Archived from the original on 18 May 2015.)*

al-Jabiri, Jamal; al-Haidari, Fawaz (19 May 2015). "UN says half a million Yemenis displaced as capital pounded". Agence France-Presse. Archivedfrom the original on 19 May 2015.

400 *al-Jabiri, Jamal; al-Haidari, Fawaz (19 May 2015). "UN says half a million Yemenis displaced as capital pounded". Agence France-Presse. Archivedfrom the original on 19 May 2015.*

"First UN flights brings emergency aid to Yemen". UNHCR. 15 May 2015. Archived from the original on 17 May 2015. (original URL: http://www.unhcr.org/55561d7b9.html)

"Huthi rebels absent as Yemeni parties gather in Riyadh". Agence France-Presse. 17 May 2015. Archived from the original on 17 May 2015.

401 *"Yemen: Humanitarian Snapshot – Displacement (as of 31 May 2015)"*. *UN Office for the Coordination of Humanitarian Affairs. 1 June 2015. Archivedfrom the original on 5 June 2015. ("PDF" (PDF). Archived from the original on 5 June 2015.)*

"Yemen: Rapid Increase in Casualties, Displacement and Scale of Destruction Flash Update 38 – 4 June 2015 (1000hrs)". UN Office for the Coordination of Humanitarian Affairs. 4 June 2015. Archived from the original on 5 June 2015. ("PDF" (PDF). Archived from the original on 5 June 2015.)

402

On 5 August, a task force of the Global Protection Cluster announced their estimate of 1,439,118 internally displaced persons from more than 250,000 households in Yemen.[403]

On 15 October the IOM-UNHCR displacement-tracking mechanism published new data showing in the 5th RFPM report that the IDP population had reached 2,305,048 people.[404]

The 6th RFPM report (published on 10 December 2015) gave a figure of 2,509,068 internally displaced persons.[405] Much of the increase from the previous report, published in October, could be attributed to improved tracking methods[406]

Starvation and diseases

On 14 June 2015, OCHA reported a large outbreak of Dengue fever that killed over 113 people and infected over 4,000. Patients could not be treated due to lack of water in affected areas. OCHA was also investigating reports of a Measles outbreak. Health officials considered the breakdown in health services, including decrease in immunization coverage, closure of health facilities and difficulty in accessing health services as possible contributing factors.[407]

In June 2015, Oxfam's humanitarian programme manager in Sanaa said that Saudi-led naval blockade "means it's impossible to bring anything into the country. There are lots of ships, with basic things like flour, that are not allowed to approach. The situation is deteriorating, hospitals are now shutting down, without diesel. People are dying of simple diseases."[408]

---

403 *"Yemen Protection Cluster:Task Force on Population Movements 4th Report, 05th August 2015"*. UN Office for the Coordination of Humanitarian Affairs, UN High Commissioner for Refugees, Protection Cluster. 5 August 2015. *Archived* from the original on 16 August 2015. *"PDF"* (PDF). *Archived*from the original on 16 August 2015.

404 *Task Force on Population Movement, 5th Report, 14 October 2015"*. UN Office for the Coordination of Humanitarian Affairs, UN High Commissioner for Refugees, Protection Cluster. 14 October 2015. *Archived* from the original on 31 October 2015. (*"original on humanitarianresponse.info"* (PDF). *Archived* from the original on 31 October 2015.)

   "Briefing Note: Despite conflict, refugees continue to arrive by boat in Yemen". UN High Commissioner for Refugees. 27 October 2015. *Archived*from the original on 29 October 2015., original: http://www.unhcr.org/562f6bba6.html unhcr.org

405 *Task Force on Population Movement, 6th Report, 10 December 2015"*. UN Office for the Coordination of Humanitarian Affairs, UN High Commissioner for Refugees, Protection Cluster. 10 December 2015. *Archived* from the original on 15 December 2015. (*"PDF"* (PDF). *Archived* from the original on 15 December 2015.)

406 *"Task Force on Population Movement, 5th Report, 14 October 2015"*. UN Office for the Coordination of Humanitarian Affairs, UN High Commissioner for Refugees, Protection Cluster. 14 October 2015. *Archived* from the original on 31 October 2015. (*"original on humanitarianresponse.info"* (PDF).

407 *"Yemen: Public Health Crisis Escalates Flash Update 39 – 14 June 2015 (1000hrs)"*. UN Office for the Coordination of Humanitarian Affairs. 14 June 2015. *Archived* from the original on 15 June 2015.

408 Borger, Julian (5 June 2015). *"Saudi-led naval blockade leaves 20 m Yemenis facing humanitarian disaster"*. *The Guardian*. Retrieved 31 October2015.

On 1 July 2015, the UN announced that Yemen was at the highest level of humanitarian disaster with over 80% of the population needing help. UN agencies agreed to classify Yemen as a level 3 emergency as the UN Envoy for Yemen stated that Yemen is one step away from famine.[409]

In February 2016, the OCHA reported that 21 million people (85% of the population) were in need of some form of humanitarian assistance, 7.6 million people were "severely" food insecure, and that more than 3.4 million children were not attending school.[410]

On 4 October 2016, the UN children's agency UNICEF said 1.5 million children in Yemen suffer of malnutrition, including 370,000 enduring very severe malnutrition.[411]

In October 2016, health authorities in Yemen confirmed a cholera outbreak in Sanaa and Taiz.[412] In June 2017, cholera cases passed 100,000 with 798 deaths in the country. The water and sanitation systems are largely inoperable[539] Numerous international humanitarian organisations have pointed to the Saudi-led naval and aerial blockade and bombing campaign as central causes behind the preventable cholera epidemic.[413]

With the right medicines, these [diseases] are all completely treatable – but the Saudi Arabia-led coalition is stopping them from getting in.

More than 50,000 children in Yemen died from starvation in 2017.[414] The number rose to 85,000 as of December 2018.[415] The famine in Yemen is the direct result of the

---

409 "UN Declares Highest-Level Humanitarian Emergency in Yemen". *The New York Times*. 1 July 2015.

410 'Humanitarian catastrophe' unfolding in Yemen: UN". Al JazeeraEnglish. 17 February 2016. Retrieved 17 February 2016.

411 "Yemen famine feared as starving children fight for lives in hospital". *The Guardian*. 4 October 2016.

412 "UN Decries Cholera Outbreak in Yemen". ABC News. 7 October 2016.

413 *Federspiel, Frederik; Ali, Mohammad (4 December 2018). "The cholera outbreak in Yemen: lessons learned and way forward". BMC Public Health. 18 (1): 1338. doi:10.1186/s12889-018-6227-6. ISSN 1471-2458. PMC 6278080. PMID 30514336.*

Bachman, Jeffrey S. (1 February 2019). "A 'synchronised attack' on life: the Saudi-led coalition's 'hidden and holistic' genocide in Yemen and the shared responsibility of the US and UK". Third World Quarterly. 40 (2): 298–316. doi:10.1080/01436597.2018.1539910. ISSN 0143-6597.

414 *editor, Patrick Wintour Diplomatic (16 November 2017). "Saudis must lift Yemen blockade or 'untold' thousands will die, UN agencies warn". The Guardian.*

Press, Associated (16 November 2017). "50,000 children in Yemen have died of starvation and disease so far this year, monitoring group says". Chicago Tribune.

415

Saudi Arabian-led intervention and blockade of Yemen.[416] In December 2017, the *Guardian* reported: "Data on coalition airstrikes collected by the Yemen Data Project have recorded 356 air raids targeting farms, 174 targeting market places and 61 air raids targeting food storage sites from March 2015 to the end of September 2017."[417]

According to the OCHA's March 2019 report, 108,889 suspected cholera and acute watery diarrhea cases were reported between January and mid-March, with one third cases of children below 5 five years. Around 190 people died in the mentioned period.[418] In August 2016, a Joint Incidents Assessment Team was formed by the coalition parties to investigate alleged laws of war violations.[419] But the team failed to meet international standards regarding transparency, impartiality, and independence. It failed to investigate and apply human rights law in the civil war and instead acted as a shield against the parties accountable for the war.[420]

In Yemen responses and Opposition

Following the call by the leader of the Houthi movement, Abdul-Malik al-Houthi, tens of thousands Yemenis of various socioeconomic backgrounds took to the streets of the rebel-controlled capital, Sana'a, to voice their anger at the Saudi intervention.[421]

On 21 April 2015, representatives of 19 Yemeni political parties and associations rejected UN Resolution 2216, stating that it encouraged terrorist expansion, intervened in Yemen's sovereign affairs, violated Yemen's right of self-defence and emphasized the associations' support of the Yemeni Army.[422]

On 23 April, a spokesman for the Houthis said UN-sponsored peace talks should continue, but only following "a complete halt of attacks" by the coalition[423]

---

416 *Kristof, Nicholas (31 August 2017). "The Photos the U.S. and Saudi Arabia Don't Want You to See". The New York Times.*

"Saudi de facto blockade starves Yemen of food and medicine". Reuters. 11 October 2017.

417 "Bombed into famine: how Saudi air campaign targets Yemen's food supplies". *The Guardian*. 12 December 2017.

418 *"YEMEN HUMANITARIAN UPDATE" (PDF). OCHA.*

419*"YEMEN HUMANITARIAN UPDATE" (PDF). OCHA.*

"Hiding Behind the Coalition". Human Rights Watch. Retrieved 24 August2018.

420 "Why Congress Must Act Now on Yemen". Human Rights Watch. Retrieved 1 April 2019.

421 Coalition jets continue to hit Houthi targets in Yemen". Al Jazeera. 27 March 2015. Retrieved 27 March 2015.

422

423 Amid Saudi Arabia's airstrikes in Yemen, Houthis call for peace talks". CNN. 23 April 2015.

In a televised address on 24 April, Saleh called on the Houthis and other armed groups to withdraw from the territory they had seized and participate in UN-sponsored peace talks, in exchange for an end to the air campaign.[424] Exiled Yemeni Foreign Minister rejected the peace proposal saying that Saleh had no role in the talks.[425]

On 26 April, the General Authority for Archeology and Museums in Yemen condemned attacks targeting historical sites. The statement highlighted an attack that completely destroyed an ancient fortress in the Damt District of the Ad Dali' Governorate.[559] Yemeni political parties issued a letter to UN Secretary-General Ban Ki-moon requesting that he continue the peace talks. The letter emphasized that Yemen was still under attack by air, land and sea and that the existing blockade was increasing the humanitarian crisis and that education had been denied for 3 million students due to the "random attacks".[426]

On 2 May 2015, the Yemenis Forum of Persons With Disability stated that 300 centres and organizations had been forced to stop operations following the intervention. The organization denounced the air and sea blockade that "increased the suffering of the disabled greatly".[561] The same day Hussein al-Ezzi, the Houthi head of foreign relations, sent a letter addressed to Secretary General Ban seeking an end to the "unjustified Saudi aggression".[562] He asked the UN to seek an end to what Houthis described as blatant aggression against the country.[427]

On 7 May, 17 humanitarian agencies stressed that life-saving aid would run out in a week and emphasized the need to remove the existing blockade. The International Non-Government Organizations Forum in Yemen appealed for allowing basic materials to enter the country immediately.[428]

On 10 May, Houthi military spokesman Sharaf Luqman welcomed the Russian initiative, which advocated a suspension of military operations and also lifting the blockade.[429]

On 26 March 2017, the second anniversary of the war, over a hundred thousand Houthi supporters demonstrated in Sanaa protesting the Saudi aggression and expressing solidarity.[430]

support

---

424 _"Yemen famine feared as starving children fight for lives in hospital"_. _The Guardian_. 4 October 2016.

425 Yemen minister rejects peace talks call from ex-president". _Reuters_. 26 April 2015.

426 https://en.wikipedia.org/wiki/Saudi_Arabian-led_intervention_in_Yemen#cite_ref-560

427 Abdullah, Khaled (2 May 2015). "Yemeni Houthis call on U.N. to end Saudi strikes: statement". _Reuters_.

428 Agencies warn of risk of preventing aid arrival to Yemen". Saba News Agency. Retrieved 11 May 2015.

429 Tezelden, Alim. "Yemen's Houthis welcome proposed Russian truce". Video News. Retrieved 11 May 2015.

430 Editorial. "Thousands of Yemenis rally in Sanaa on war's second anniversary". _Reuters_. Retrieved 29 June 2018.

Anti-Houthi groups, especially Sunnis, while supporting the intervention did not wish for the return to power of Hadi, since they viewed him as the man "who ceded control of the capital without a fight six months ago".[431]

On 3 April, the Al-Islah party, the Yemeni branch of the Muslim Brotherhood, declared its support for the campaign.[432] Supporters of the party reportedly suffered consequences, including kidnappings and raids, as a result of this declaration.[433]

On 26 April, the foreign minister in Hadi's government, Riad Yaseen, rejected Saleh's calls for UN-sponsored peace talks on the ground[434]

Opposition

On 5 April a firefight broke out between anti-government Shiite rioters and security forces in Saudi Arabia's Shiite-minority in Eastern Province, with one police officer killed and three others injured.[435] The firefight broke out after calls in the Eastern Province to protest against the military intervention.[436]

On 29 April, King Salman dismissed his appointed crown prince, Muqrin of Saudi Arabia. Some regional political analysts speculated that the decision was precipitated by Muqrin's alleged opposition to the intervention. Salman appointed Muhammad bin Nayef, who publicly announced his support of the operation, to replace Muqrin.[437]

---

431 "OIC supports military action in Yemen". *Arab News*. 27 March 2015.

432 "Yemen's Houthis quit Aden palace after Saudi strikes". Middle East Eye. 3 April 2015.

433 al-Mujahed, Ali (5 April 2015). *"Yemen rebels stage raids on suspected opponents amid Saudi-led airstrikes"*. *The Washington Post*.

"Saudi-led bombing campaign deepens rifts in Yemen". *Middle East Eye*. 10 April 2015

434 "Yemeni foreign minister rejects peace talks call from ex-president". *Reuters*. 26 April 2015. Police officer killed in security raids on Saudi Arabia's Eastern Province". One police officer was killed and three others injured on Sunday in Saudi Arabia's Eastern Province, as government forces clashed with locals, according to a Ministry of Interior statement.

435

436 Police officer killed in security raids on Saudi Arabia's Eastern Province". The latest round of clashes in Awamiyah on Sunday came after calls in the province for protests against Saudi Arabia's military intervention in Yemen, where Riyadh is battling to push back Shiite Houthi rebels who have expanded their powerbase to the capital Sanaa and beyond, forcing the sitting president into exile.

437 *"Saudi king names new heir in sign of toughening regional stance"*. *The Miami Herald*. 29 April 2015. Retrieved 1 May 2015.

"Yemen's War Shakes Up the Saudi Palace"

Support

On 21 April, Saudi prince Al-Waleed bin Talal reportedly offered 100 Bentleys to participating pilots. The announcement was met with substantial criticism.[438]

Among the general populace, the war was popular.[439]

Other coalition countries

Bahrain[

King Hamad bin Isa Al Khalifa of Bahrain in 2015

On 3 April Bahrainis protested against the war on Yemen.[440] A prominent Bahraini opposition politician, Fadhel Abbas, was reportedly arrested by Bahraini authorities for condemning the bombing as "flagrant aggression".[441]

Egypt

Supporters of the Egyptian Muslim Brotherhood demonstrated against Egypt's military intervention.[442]

Kuwait

Shiite parliament member Abdul Hamid Dashti reportedly criticized the war and described it as an "act of aggression".[443]Kuwaiti authorities for his criticism of the Saudi government summoned a prominent Shiite lawyer, Khalid Al Shatti.[444]

---

438 Saul, Heather (23 April 2015). "Saudi Prince Al-Waleed bin Talal faces backlash for 'promising Bentleys to fighter pilots bombing Yemen'". *The Independent*. London. A Saudi Prince has come under fire on social media after reportedly promising luxury Bentley cars to fighter pilots involved in bombing strikes in Yemen.

439 "Saudi Arabia: The challenged kingdom". *The Economist*. 23 May 2015. Retrieved 31 May 2015.

440 Mackey, Robert (3 April 2015). "Bahrain Arrests Rights Activist Over Tweets About Torture". *The New York Times*. Protesters in Bahrain on Friday denounced the military intervention in Yemen, holding up posters of Abdul-Malik al-Houthi, the rebel leader who comes from the Zaydi sect, an offshoot of Shiite Islam.

441 Mackey, Robert (3 April 2015). "Bahrain Arrests Rights Activist Over Tweets About Torture". *The New York Times*. Last week, Bahrain's police force announced the arrest of an opposition politician, Fadhel Abbas, and an associate for supposedly disturbing the peace with a statement posted on Twitter that condemned the bombing of Yemen as "flagarent aggression" that violated international law.

442 Muslim Brotherhood split on Saudi strikes in Yemen". Al-Monitor. Most of the reactions were clear, with the exception of the Brotherhood's, whose Yemeni branch supported the operation and Egyptian branch rejected it. Regardless of the Brotherhood's views on Egypt's participation, they were criticized by their supporters who held demonstrations opposing military action

443 فريق , لتحرير (21 April 2015). "الكويت : فيديو .. نائب كويتي يصف عاصفة الحزم بالعدوان".

444 Madeleine Wells (13 April 2015). "Sectarianism and authoritarianism in Kuwait". *The Washington Post*. Retrieved 24 April 2015.

On 28 April, Kuwaiti Foreign Minister Sabah Al-Khalid Al-Sabah stated that the only solution to the Yemen crisis was political[445]

International

International reactions to the Saudi-led intervention in Yemen (2015–present)

Foreign Ministers of the U.S., the U.K., Saudi Arabia and the United Arab Emirates, before a working dinner focused on Yemen, 19 July 2016

The Arab League, United States, Turkey, OIC and Hamas voiced support for the intervention[446]but the European Union, Russia[447]and the United Nations criticised it.[448] The United Kingdom, and France supported the intervention,[449] and along with Canada have supplied the Saudi military with equipment.[450]

---

445 "KUNA : Political solution in Yemen is only solution – Kuwaiti FM – Politics". kuna.net.kw. 28 April 2015.

446 Boyle, Christina; al-Alayaa, Zaid (29 March 2015). *"Arab League's joint military force is a 'defining moment' for region"*. *Los Angeles Times*. Retrieved 3 April 2015.

"Turkey supports Saudi mission in Yemen, says Iran must withdraw". *France 24*. 26 March 2015.

"Hamas supports military operation for political legitimacy in Yemen". Arab News. 30 March 2015.

"OIC supports military action in Yemen". *Arab News. 27 March 2015.*

447 *"Iraq PM says Yemen could stoke regional war, slams Saudi operations"*. *Reuters.* 15 April 2015.

448 *"EU warns of serious regional consequences of Yemeni crisis"*. *Laprensasa. 29 March 2015. Retrieved 29 March 2015.*

Sharkov, Damien (30 March 2015). *"Saudi Arabia Accuse Putin of Hypocrisy After Letter to Arab League"*. *Newsweek. Retrieved 3 April 2015.*

"Senior UN officials deeply concerned over civilian casualties in wake of recent fighting in Yemen". *UN News Centre. 31 March 2015. Retrieved 3 April 2015.*

449 "France voices support for Saudi campaign in Yemen". France 24. 12 April 2015.

450 *Coughlin, Con (23 April 2015). "Yemen crisis: British MPs clash over supplying bombs to Saudi Arabia as coalition launches new air strikes"*. *The Daily Telegraph. London.*

"Human rights groups ask Trudeau to end 'immoral' arms deal with Saudi Arabia". *The Globe and Mail. 27 April 2016.*

"Arms sales to Saudi 'illicit' due to civilian deaths in Yemen: campaigners". Reuters. 22 August 2016.

Iran condemned intervention as "US-backed aggression".[451]Iran's U.N. Ambassador Gholamali Khoshroo said that "those who violate international law, including international humanitarian law, should be held accountable for their acts and there should be no room for impunity."[452] Iraqi Prime Minister Haidar al-Abadi expressed the Iraqi government's opposition to the intervention: "This (Yemen war) can engulf the whole region in another conflict. We don't need another sectarian war in the region."[453] The Hezbollah secretary general criticized Saudi Arabia and its allies, saying "all invaders end up being defeated".[454]

The Chinese foreign ministry expressed in January 2016 its support for the intervention and the Hadi government, while stressing its desire for a resumption of stability in Yemen.[455]

Somalia's government blamed the Saudi-led coalition for the killing of at least 42 Somali refugees off the Yemeni coast. Somali Prime Minister Hassan Ali Khayre called the attack on a boat carrying refugees "atrocious" and "appalling".[456]

According to Russia's state-controlled channel *RT*, "many Americans are not even aware of Yemen's plight, even less so of America's role in it. The US not only arms the Saudis, but also provides air refueling and targeting for their warplanes. ... The American people are not to be blamed though. When their media consider *"Russiagate"* stories 50 times more newsworthy than the situation in Yemen, it takes a curious mind to become aware."[457]

Asian countries including China, India, Malaysia and Pakistan, moved within days to evacuate their citizens from Yemen.[458]

---

451 *"Iraq PM says Yemen could stoke regional war, slams Saudi operations"*. *Reuters*. 15 April 2015.

452 "Iran complains to UN of foiled Yemen aid as ship standoff looms". Reuters. 13 May 2015.

453 *"Iraq PM says Yemen could stoke regional war, slams Saudi operations"*. *Reuters*. 15 April 2015.

454 *"Hizballah chief criticises Saudi Arabia for Yemen intervention"*. *Retrieved 5 March 2016*.

455 https://www.reuters.com/article/us-saudi-china-yemen/china-offers-support-for-yemen-government-as-xi-visits-saudi-arabia-idUSKCN0UY0C1, 20 January 2016

456 "Saudi-led coalition blamed after helicopter gunship massacres Somali refugees". *The Independent*. 18 March 2017.

457 3 years of Yemen bloodbath marked by US & UK arms deals with Saudis". RT. 26 March 2018.

458 *Browning, Noah (29 March 2015). "Chinese warship docks in Aden to evacuate nationals – port official". Reuters. Retrieved 3 April 2015.*

Mahadzir, Dzirhan (9 April 2015). "Malaysia sends C-130s for Yemen evacuation". Jane's Information Group. Archived from the original on 17 April 2015. Retrieved 18 April 2015.

Pakistan evacuates hundreds during pause in Yemen strikes – Saudi official". Reuters. 29 March 2015. Retrieved 29 March 2015.

Peri, Dinakar; Phadnis, Renuka (3 April 2015). "India begins evacuating citizens". The Hindu. Chennai, India. Retrieved 3 April 2015.

On 4 April, the ICRC called for a 24-hour humanitarian ceasefire after the coalition blocked three aid shipments to Yemen.[506] Russia also called for "humanitarian pauses" in the coalition bombing campaign, bringing the idea before the United Nations Security Council in a 4 April emergency meeting.[459] Saudi Arabia's UN ambassador raised questions over whether humanitarian pauses are the best way of delivering humanitarian assistance.[460] On 7 April, China renewed calls for an immediate ceasefire[461]

On 10 April, the Pakistani Parliament declined a Saudi Arabian request to join the coalition. The Parliament clarified the wish to maintain a neutral diplomatic stance.[462]

On 16 April a group of US and UK-based Yemen scholars wrote an open letter, stating that the operation was illegal under international law and calling for the UN to enforce an immediate ceasefire.[463]

On 19 April, international aid agency Oxfam condemned SA over airstrikes it said hit one of its warehouses containing humanitarian supplies in Saada.[464]

Aid groups came out against the air campaign: Amnesty International said some of the coalition's airstrikes "appear to have failed to take necessary precautions to minimize harm to civilians and damage to civilian objects".[465] Reporters without Borders condemned a strike in Sanaa on 20 April that caused the deaths of four employees of Al-Yemen Al-Youm TV and injured ten others; it also condemned attacks on journalists by pro-Houthi forces.[466]

On 4 May the UN called on the coalition to stop attacking Sanaa Airport to allow delivery of humanitarian aid.[467] On 10 May the UN Humanitarian Coordinator for Yemen stated that the attacks on Saada province were in breach of international law.[468] On 29 June,

---

459 Lederer, Edith (4 April 2015). "Russia Urges UN to Call for 'Humanitarian Pause' in Yemen". ABC News.

460 "Russia calls for pause in Yemen air strikes to evacuate foreigners". Reuters UK. 4 April 2015.

461 "China calls for ceasefire in Yemen". Retrieved 15 April 2015.

462 Pakistan declines Saudi call for armed support in Yemen fight". Reuters. 10 April 2015. Retrieved 15 April 2015.

463 Tharoor, Ishaan (18 April 2015). "Top Yemen scholars in the West condemn Saudi Arabia's war". The Washington Post – Blogs. Archived from the original on 19 April 2015.

464 "Aid agency Oxfam condemns Saudi air strike in Yemen". Reuters. 20 April 2015.

465 Yemen: Relentless airstrikes that have left hundreds of civilians dead must be investigated". Amnesty International. 24 April 2014

466 Journalists Killed, Injured as Security Situation Worsens". Reporters without Borders. 24 April 2015. Journalists Killed, Injured as Security Situation Worsens". Reporters without Borders. 24 April 2015.

467 "UPDATE 1-UN urges Saudi-led coalition to stop targeting Yemen airport". Reuters. 4 May 2015.

468 Malaysian forces join Saudi-led coalition in Yemen". i24news. Retrieved 11 May 2015.

Secretary General Ban Ki-moon denounced a coalition airstrike that had hit a UN compound in Aden the previous day and requested a full investigation.[469]

UN Secretary-General Ban Ki-moon has criticized Saudi Arabian-led intervention in Yemen

Human Rights Watch criticized the UN Security Council repeatedly for "remaining almost silent on coalition abuses".[470]In January 2016 an unpublished United Nations panel investigating the Saudi-led bombing campaign in Yemen uncovered "widespread and systematic" attacks on civilian targets in violation of international humanitarian law, calling UN Security Council up for an international commission of inquiry[471]Saudi Arabia had previously objected to an inquiry being set up,[472] and had not been supported by Western governments.[473]

In February 2016 the Secretary-General of the UN (UNSG) Ban Ki-moon raised strong concerns over continued Saudi-led airstrikes, saying that "coalition air strikes in particular continue to strike hospitals, schools, mosques and civilian infrastructures" in Yemen. He urged States that are signatories to the Arms Trade Treaty to "control arms flows to actors that may use them in ways that breach of international humanitarian law".[474]

---

469   "United Nations News Centre". UN News Service Section. 29 June 2015. Retrieved 13 July 2015.

470 "UN: Most Attacks on Yemen Civilians From Saudi-Led Coalition". *The New York Times*. Associated Press. 22 December 2015. Archived from the original on 24 December 2015.

471 *MacAskill, Ewen (27 January 2016). "UN report into Saudi-led strikes in Yemen raises questions over UK role – Experts conclude Saudi-led coalition conducted widespread airstrikes against civilian targets in violation of international law". The Guardian. Archived from the original on 28 January 2016.*

"UN Panel Alleges Violations of International Law in Yemen". Voice of America. 26 January 2016. Archived from the original on 28 January 2016.

472 "UN resolution on Yemen fails to launch international investigation into war crimes". Amnesty International. 2 October 2015. Archived from the original on 8 October 2015.

473 *Sengupta, Somini (22 December 2015). "Saudi-Led War in Yemen Frays Ties With the U.S." The New York Times. Archived from the original on 24 December 2015.*

Oakford, Samuel (7 January 2016). "The UN's Top Human Rights Official in Yemen is Now 'Persona Non Grata'". Vice News. Retrieved 28 January2016.

Chandler, Adam (2 October 2015). "Looking the Other Way in Yemen – The U.S. allowed the Saudis to block a UN inquiry into the thousands of deaths in Yemen's civil war". The Atlantic. Archived from the original on 19 October 2015.

474 *Secretary-General's address at event co-organized by the United Nations Association of the United Kingdom and Chatham House". un.org (UNSG Ban Ki-moon). 5 February 2016. Archived from the original on 8 February 2016.*

In June 2016, Ban Ki-moon removed a Saudi-led coalition from a list of children's rights violators,[475] saying that Saudi Arabia threatened to cut Palestinian aid and funds to other UN programs if coalition was not removed from blacklist for killing children in Yemen. According to one source, there was also a threat of "clerics in Riyadh meeting to issue a fatwa against the UN, declaring it anti-Muslim, which would mean no contacts of OIC members, no relations, contributions, support, to any UN projects, programs".[476]

In September 2016, British Foreign Secretary Boris Johnson was accused of blocking the UN inquiry into Saudi war crimes in Yemen.[477]

In April 2018, French President Emmanuel Macron voiced support for the Saudi Arabian-led intervention in Yemen and defended France's arms sales to the Saudi-led coalition.[478]

Bahri Abha – the Saudi Arabian ship arrived on 10 December 2019, at the Sagunto, Valencia port, where they were faced by Spanish Control Arms campaign organizations. Since the beginning of the Yemen war, the same ship has reportedly ferried $162 million worth of US-made arms to the kingdom. The organizations of the likes of Amnesty International, FundiPau, Greenpeace and Oxfam Intermón have objected to the shipment of arms from Spanish port[479]

al-Qaeda insurgency in Yemen

Both al-Qaeda in the Arabian Peninsula (AQAP) and Islamic State had a presence in Yemen before the Saudi-led intervention. AQAP had controlled substantial pieces of territory for some time, while Islamic State claimed for twin bombings in Sanaa the following month that killed 140 people and injured hundreds more[480]

The two radical groups have used the conflict to expand and consolidate, an obvious fact accepted by the Pentagon.[481] The Houthis disengaged fighting AQAP to face

---

"Yemen – Conflict (ECHO, UN, Media) (ECHO Daily Flash of 8 February 2016". European Commission Humanitarian Aid Office. 8 February 2016. *Archived* from the original on 8 February 2016. (*"original"*. *Archived* from the original on 8 February 2016.)

475 United Nations Chief Exposes Limits to His Authority by Citing Saudi Threat". *The New York Times*. 8 June 2016.

476 "Saudi Arabian allies pressured UN chief to issue blacklist reversal, sources say". *The Guardian*. 8 June 2016.

477 "Boris Johnson criticised by human rights groups after blocking inquiry into war crimes in Yemen". *The Independent*. 27 September 2016.

478 "France's Macron defends Saudi arms sales, to hold Yemen conference". Reuters. 10 April 2018.

479 Spain: Ensure Saudi Arabian ship carries no arms through Spanish ports". *Amnesty International*. Retrieved 10 December 2019.

480 Mendelsohn, Barak (21 March 2015). "Islamic State in Yemen: Why IS is seeking to expand". *BBC News*. Retrieved 24 February 2016.

rival Yemeni militias at the same time as they were being hit by coalition air strikes;[482] A source indicates that Yemeni troops in the south remained in their bases instead of confronting al-Qaeda militants, fearing Saudi air strikes on any troop movements.[483] There are questions about the ability of the country to confront its Islamist militancy problem due to the major infrastructure damage caused by the war.[484]

Within weeks of the commencement of the Yemen's civil war, AQAP had exploited the chaos to capture the south-eastern port city of Mukalla,[485] along with nearby military, transport, and economic infrastructure.[486] A series of prison breaks by al-Qaeda—they emptied Mukalla's jail of 300 prisoners and emptied 1,200 inmates in June 2015 from the central prison in Taiz—released jailed jihadists of all ranks.[487] Reports indicate that Yemen's prisons had, in preceding years, reportedly become "de facto jihadi academies", as veteran militants were placed in cells alongside young, regular criminals.[488]

The coalition campaign against the Houthis in Yemen's city of Aden in July 2015 and subsequent chaos increased AQAP and Islamic State presence in the city.[489] Residents

---

481 Al-batati, Saeed; Fahim, Kareem (16 April 2015). "War in Yemen Is Allowing Qaeda Group to Expand". *The New York Times*. Retrieved 24 February 2016.

482 *Al-batati, Saeed; Fahim, Kareem (16 April 2015). "War in Yemen Is Allowing Qaeda Group to Expand". The New York Times. Retrieved 24 February 2016.*

Salisbury, Peter (28 October 2014). "The Houthis Are Battling al Qaeda Amid a 'Slow-Burning Coup' in Yemen". Vice News. Retrieved 24 February 2016. [T]hey are deadly serious about eradicating AQAP [...] the group's desire to break AQAP's grip on the north of the country remains undimmed.

483 Johnsen, Gregory D. (2 April 2015). "Al-Qaeda Commander Freed in Yemen Prison Break". BuzzFeed. Retrieved 4 February 2016.

484 Johnsen, Gregory D. (2 April 2015). "Al-Qaeda Commander Freed in Yemen Prison Break". BuzzFeed. Retrieved 4 February 2016.

485 Kirkpatrick, David D.; Fahim, Kareem (2 April 2015). "Saudi Leaders Have High Hopes for Yemen Airstrikes, but Houthi Attacks Continue". *The New York Times*. Retrieved 4 April 2015.

486 *Al-batati, Saeed; Fahim, Kareem (16 April 2015). "War in Yemen Is Allowing Qaeda Group to Expand". The New York Times. Retrieved 24 February 2016.*

487 *Alexander, Harriet (2 April 2015). "Al-Qaeda frees 300 prisoners in Yemen jail break". The Daily Telegraph. Retrieved 4 February 2016.*

"Around 1,200 escape from Yemen prison, including al Qaeda suspects". Reuters. 30 June 2015. Retrieved 4 February 2016.

488 Johnsen, Gregory D. (2 April 2015). "Al-Qaeda Commander Freed in Yemen Prison Break". BuzzFeed. Retrieved 4 February 2016.

489 Gardner, Frank (2 September 2015). "Has Yemen war handed Aden to jihadists?". *BBC News*. Retrieved 24 February 2016.

of Aden faced a wave of bombings and shootings that prevented efforts at stabilization.[490] AQAP conducted assassinations of judges, security officials, and police.[491]

On 26 August 2015, Bob Semple, a British petroleum engineer who was kidnapped and held as a hostage by Al Qaeda in Yemen was freed by the UAE armed forces after 18 months of captivity.[492]

At the start of February 2016, AQAP recaptured Azzan, an important commercial city in Shabwa province.[493] A few weeks later, al-Qaeda fighters and Saudi-led coalition forces were seen fighting a common target; the Houthis.[494] But the situation is different in Aden, the AQAP/ISIS and pro-Hadi that were fighting a common enemy in Taiz are enemies in Aden. On 29 February 2016, a suicide car killed 4 pro-Hadi troops in Shiek Othman district in Aden, the city that Hadi uses as a temporary capital.[495]

The United Arab Emirates has spearheaded an active role against fighting AQAP and ISIL-YP presence in Yemen through a partnership with the United States.[496] In April 2016, UAE armed forces assisted Yemeni forces in retaking the city of Mukalla from AQAP during the Battle of Mukalla.[497] In August 2017, the UAE armed forces assisted a Yemeni army offensive against AQAP in Shabwah Governorate.[498]

In an Op-Ed in *The Washington Post* Yousef Al Otaiba, the UAE ambassador to the United States, described that the intervention has reduced AQAP presence in Yemen to its weakest point since 2012 with many areas previously under their control liberated.[499] The ambassador declared that more than 2,000 militants have been removed from the battlefield, with their controlled areas now having improved

---

490 *"Yemen clashes kill 6, including 4 family members"*. Agence France-Presse. 9 February 2016. Archived from the original on 10 February 2016.

491 Ghobari, Mohammed; Bayoumy, Yara (9 February 2016). "Wave of Aden killings tests Gulf role in Yemen". Reuters. Archived from the original on 10 February 2016.

492 "Freed British hostage pays tribute to UAE". emirates246. Retrieved 7 September 2015.

493 Asher-Schapiro, Avi (1 February 2016). "Al Qaeda Is Making Serious Gains Amid Chaos of Yemen's Civil War". Vice News. Retrieved 24 February 2016

494 "Yemen conflict: Al-Qaeda joins coalition battle for Taiz". *BBC News*. 22 February 2016. Retrieved 23 February 2016.

495

496 Ardemagni, Eleonora (28 July 2016). "Uae's military priorities in Yemen: Counterterrorism and the South". *.ispionline.it*.

497 *Yemeni Troops, Backed by United Arab Emirates, Take City From Al Qaeda"*. *The New York Times*. 24 April 2016.

2. ^ *"The Giant Al Qaeda Defeat That No One's Talking About"*. *Politico*. 2 May 2016.

498 "US puts boots on the ground in Yemen to attack AQAP". *Military Times*. 4 August 2017.

security and a better delivered humanitarian and development assistance such as to the port city of Mukalla and other liberated areas.[500] An Associated Press investigation outlined that the military coalition in Yemen actively reduced AQAP in Yemen without military intervention, instead by offering them deals and even actively recruiting them in the coalition because "they are considered as exceptional fighters".[648] UAE Brigadier General Musallam Al Rashidi responded to the accusations by stating that Al Qaeda cannot be reasoned with and cited that multiple of his soldiers have been killed by them.[501] The UAE military stated that accusations of allowing AQAP to leave with cash contradict their primary objective of depriving AQAP of its financial strength.[502] The notion of the coalition recruiting or paying AQAP has been thoroughly denied by the United States Pentagon with Colonel Robert Manning, spokesperson of the Pentagon, calling the news source "patently false".[503] The governor of Hadramut Faraj al-Bahsani, dismissed the accusations that Al Qaeda has joined with the coalition rank, explaining that if they did there would be sleeper cells and that he would be "the first one to be killed". According to *The Independent*, AQAP activity on social media as well as the number of terror attacks conducted by them has decreased since the Emirati intervention.[504]

In January 2019, CNN stated that Saudi Arabia and the UAE provided al-Qaeda linked groups in Yemen with US-made military equipment including vehicles.[505]

On 25 June 2019, Saudi special forces announced that they captured the leader of the ISIL-YP, Abu Osama al-Muhajer, on the 3 June along with other members including the chief financial officer of the organization.[506]

In April 2020, Yemeni journalist Salah Bin Laghbar revealed documents showing cooperation between Saudi-led coalition and al-Qaeda in Yemen; "An official

---

499 "The Arab coalition is making progress against extremists in Yemen". *The Washington Post*. 12 September 2018.

500 "The Arab coalition is making progress against extremists in Yemen". *The Washington Post*. 12 September 2018.

501 UAE responds to AP report on deals with al-Qaida in Yemen". Associated Press. 13 August 2018.

502 Trew, Bel (15 August 2018). "Inside the UAE's war on al-Qaeda in Yemen". *The Independent*.

503 "Pentagon denies reports of U.S. allies bribing, recruiting al Qaeda fighters in Yemen". *The Washington Times*. Retrieved 29 August 2018.

504 Trew, Bel (15 August 2018). "Inside the UAE's war on al-Qaeda in Yemen". *The Independent*.

505 "Saudi Arabia, UAE gave US arms to al-Qaeda-linked groups: Report". www.aljazeera.com.

"US arms sold to Saudi Arabia and UAE end up in wrong hands". www.cnn.com.

506 Saudi forces say they have captured leader of Yemen branch of Islamic State". *Reuters*. 25 June 2019.

document from the al-Humiqani tribe warns Saudi-led coalition against sending weapons to terrorist organizations through the Al-Rashad Party, Muslim Brotherhood and terrorist Abdul Rahman Abu al-Harith al-Humiqani, who is affiliated with Daesh."[507]

On 25 March, Gulf Air, the Bahraini flag carrier airline announced the immediate suspension of service to Sanaʻa.[508] Somali airlines such as Daallo Airlines and Jubba Airways also encountered difficulties, as they were unable to fly over Yemen after its airspace became restricted.[509] On 15 April, Turkish Airlines suspended all Yemen flights until 1 June.[510]

Following Hadi's request, the administration of the Egypt-based Nilesat and Saudi-based Arabsat, two satellite communication companies, stopped broadcasting Yemeni state-run television channels that had fallen under Houthi control. The channels included Al-Yemen, Al-Eman, Saba News Agency and Aden TV. Armed Houthis closed down the Sanaʻa offices of four media outlets, including Al Jazeera, Yemen Shabab and Suhail channels, as well as Al-Masdar's newspaper and website. Al-Saeeda channel was also stormed, but was allowed to remain open on the condition it not broadcast anti-Houthi material. Houthi Political Office member Mohammad Al-Bukhaiti said the channels were closed for supporting the coalition.[511]

King Salman replaced his half-brother Muqrin as crown prince with Muhammad bin Nayef and named his son Mohammed bin Salman as defence minister, and then-Ambassador to the United States Adel al-Jubeir as foreign minister. Some reports linked the cabinet reshuffle to the war.[512] At least one political analyst suggested that Muqrin was not supportive of the military intervention, and that this cost him his

---

507 https://www.middleeastmonitor.com/20200409-yemen-document-exposes-saudi-coalition-support-for-al-qaeda-in-baydah

508 "Gulf Air suspends Sana'a service due to worsening security". *Air Transport World*. 25 March 2015. Retrieved 25 March 2015.

509 "Saudi Arabia airstrikes in Yemen disrupt Somalia flights". Garowe Online. 26 March 2015. Retrieved 26 March 2015.

510 Turkish Airlines suspends Yemen flights". Andalou Agency. 15 April 2015.

511 "Deadly Strikes Hit Yemen for Fourth Night". *Yemen Times*. 29 March 2015. Retrieved 30 March 2015.

512 *Riedel, Bruce (29 April 2015). "Yemen's War Shakes Up the Saudi Palace". The Daily Beast. Retrieved 30 April 2015.*

Maclean, William (29 April 2015). "Saudi foreign minister is Washington insider, confidant of king". Reuters. Retrieved 30 April 2015.

position.[513] Prince Muqrin's Yemeni Lineage was pointed out as another possible cause.[514]

The exiled Yemeni government sent a request to the UN, asking for foreign troops on the ground.[515]

On 19 June, WikiLeaks announced the intention of releasing over 500,000 Saudi diplomatic documents to the internet. In its statement, WikiLeaks referred to a recent electronic attack on the Saudi Foreign Ministry by a group calling itself the Yemen Cyber Army, but did not indicate whether they passed the documents to WikiLeaks.[516]

Yemeni peace process

Peace talks - Cease fire talks

On 15 May 2015, new UN envoy to Yemen Ismail Ould Cheikh Ahmed proposed peace talks in Geneva. Rebel spokesman Hamed al-Bokheiti said the Houthis were willing to hold talks in any "neutral" country.[517] Five days later the Secretary-General of the United Nations, Ban Ki-moon announced that peace talks would be held in Geneva starting on 28 May and urged all parties to participate.[518] Houthi rebels reiterated their support for the talks while exiled government officials said they would participate only if the Houthi's withdrew from occupied cities.[519]

On 26 May, Ban announced that the peace talks were to be postponed indefinitely after exiled Yemeni officials refused to attend until rebels withdrew from all occupied cities.[520] On 6 June the UN announced that peace talks would take place on 14 June[521]Both the exiled officials and the Houthi group confirmed their attendance.[522]

513 Hussain, Tom (28 April 2015). *"Saudi king, facing challenges in Yemen, fires his heir, foreign minister"*. *The News Tribune*. Tacoma, Wash. Archived from the original on 30 April 2015. Retrieved 30 April 2015.

514 Varghese, Johnlee (29 April 2015). *"'Political Earthquake' in Saudi Arabia: Prince Muqrin's Yemeni Lineage Cost him the Crown?"*. *International Business Times*. Retrieved 2 May 2015

515 Shaheen, Kareem (7 May 2015). "Yemen's exiled government asks UN for ground troops to halt Houthi advance" – via www.theguardian.com.

516 "WikiLeaks says it's leaking over 500,000 Saudi documents". *The Times of India*. Retrieved 29 July 2015.

517 "Middle East updates / Clashes in Yemen mar truce as UN envoy pushes for talks". *Haaretz*. 15 May 2015. Retrieved 18 May 2015

518 "Yemen conflict: UN to sponsor peace talks in Geneva". *BBC News*.

519 *"Saudi Arabia 'rejects Israeli offer to supply Iron Dome'"*. *The Times of Israel*.

520 "John Kerry says Yemen's Houthis and Saudi coalition agree to ceasefire". *The Guardian*. 15 November 2016. Retrieved 17 November 2016.

521 Nichols, Michelle (6 June 2015). "U.N. to convene Yemen peace talks on June 14". *Reuters*. Retrieved 13 July 2015.

522 Yemen's Houthis agree to talks as bombing reportedly kills 58 people". *Reuters*. 5 June 2015. Retrieved 13 July 2015.

15–19 June 2015 talks

Secretary-General Ban called for a "humanitarian pause" during the Muslim holy month of Ramadan. Peace talks between the exiled government and the Houthis concluded in Geneva without reaching a ceasefire.[523]

Ramadan peace agreement

On 4 July 2015, Houthi spokesman Mohammed Abdul Salam said in a post on his Facebook page that he had met Ahmed on Friday to discuss a Ramadan truce. The US and EU announced their support for a humanitarian truce[524]

On 9 July, the UN announced an unconditional truce between 10 July until the end of Eid ul Fitr on 17 July. The Special Envoy to Yemen assured the agreement of all warring factions.[674] The truce was interrupted within an hour by airstrikes.[675] Coalition spokesman later added that the coalition was not bound by the truce and that any truce would be counterproductive.[676] It later added that it was not requested to pause by the exiled Yemeni Government.[677]

Further peace talks

On 8 September 2015, Vice News revealed a leaked email by UN Envoy to Yemen Ismail Ould Cheikh Ahmed. In it, the envoy confirms that Houthi rebels and the party of former president and Houthi ally Ali Abdullah Saleh have expressed willingness to accept—with some reservations—a UN Security Council resolution, approved in April. This demanded the rebels "withdraw their forces from all areas they have seized, including the capital, Sanaa". "AA/GPC agreed to a new wording on UNSC resolution 2216 that states unequivocally that they are committed to the implementation of 2216 (see document attached) with the exception of article which infringe on Yemeni sovereignty and those related to sanctions," wrote Ould Cheikh Ahmed, referring to Ansar Allah (AA)—another name for the Houthis—and Saleh's General People's Congress party (GPC). "In addition, the new text includes acceptance of the return of the current government for a period of 60 days during which a government of national unity shall be formed," wrote the envoy in the email. According to Ould Cheikh Ahmed, during talks, the Houthis gave ground on certain language, including "mandatory support by the international community for reconstruction that was in the earlier version". "The latter was particularly opposed by KSA Kingdom of Saudi Arabia and GCC Gulf Cooperation Council who did not want it to be interpreted as a form of mandatory compensation," added the UN envoy[525]

On 10 September, UN Envoy to Yemen announced that all parties had agreed to peace talks. A statement from Hadi's office following a meeting on the issue of new talks affirmed the president's "complete support for the sincere efforts exerted by the

---

523 *"Talks on Yemen war end without agreement"*. *Dawn*. Pakistan. 20 June 2015. Retrieved 20 June 2015.

Chanda, Abikh (15 June 2015). *"Ban calls for immediate humanitarian truce in Yemen"*. *The Daily Star*. Lebanon. Retrieved 20 June 2015

524 "Yemen's Houthis say Ramadan humanitarian pause under discussion". *Reuters*. 4 July 2015. Retrieved 13 July 2015.

525 "Leaked UN Email on Yemen Shows Difficulty of Negotiations – and Fears Over Al Qaeda's Growing Presence". Vice News. Retrieved 15 November 2015.

special envoy". It urged Ahmed to "exert efforts to achieve the public and honest commitment on the part of the Houthis and Saleh" to implement 14 April council resolution unconditionally.[526] On 13 September, the exiled Yemeni government announced that it would no longer participate in the peace talks.[527]

2016 talks

On 18 April, peace talks aimed at ending Yemen's civil war that were set to begin faltered before they could start, when delegates representing Yemen's Houthi rebels refused to attend.[528]

On 20 April, talks convened, based on UN Security Council resolution 2216 which called for the Houthi fighters to withdraw from areas they seized since 2014 and hand heavy weapons back to the government.[529]

On 6 August, the UN special envoy to Yemen, Ismail Ould Cheikh Ahmed, announced the suspension in Kuwait, where the talks were being held. He said that the negotiations were not a failure and that they would resume in a month at an undisclosed location. Mr. Ahmed is the second United Nations envoy to try to broker peace talks between the Houthis and other factions in Yemen since March 2015. His predecessor quit after similar peace talk efforts failed. After the breakdown of the talks, one of the Houthi negotiators, Nasser Bagazgooz, blamed the United Nations envoy for seeking what he said amounted to a military solution on behalf of the Saudi-led coalition.[530] Previous negotiations floated the idea of forming a unity government—composed of Houthi and former Hadi government leaders. But the exiled Hadi leaders have consistently rejected any deal that would diminish their power over Yemen, and the Houthis have said that they will reject any deal that does not give them a seat at the table.[531]

---

526 "UN envoy announces new Yemen peace talks next week". *U.S. News & World Report*. Retrieved 15 November 2015.

527 Almasmari, Hakim (13 September 2015). "As U.N. Yemen talks near, President pulls out". CNN. Retrieved 15 November 2015.

528 *Al-batati, Saeed; Fahim, Kareem (18 April 2016). "Yemen Peace Effort Falters as Houthis Refuse to Attend Talks". The New York Times. Retrieved 13 August 2016.*

529 *"UN Yemen envoy hails 'constructive' peace talks". Al Jazeera. Retrieved 13 August 2016.*

530 Varghese, Johnlee (29 April 2015). "'Political Earthquake' in Saudi Arabia: Prince Muqrin's Yemeni Lineage Cost him the Crown?". *International Business Times*. Retrieved 2 May 2015.

531 *Emmons2016-08-11T18:45:04+00:00, Alex EmmonsAlex. "Lopsided Peace Talks Collapse, Saudis Resume Bombing Yemen and U.S. Sells More Weapons". The Intercept. Retrieved 13 August 2016.*

"Yemen peace talks stuck in stalemate". Al-Monitor. 20 May 2016. Retrieved 13 August 2016.

"Houthis demand 'unity' president as part of Yemen peace deal". Retrieved 13 August 2016.

November Ceasefire

The Saudi-led military coalition and Houthis (Ansar Allah) arrived at a swift ceasefire agreement effective 17 November 2016, as a result of efforts of US Secretary of State John Kerry and Omani dignitaries.[532]

Yemeni civil war - Why are the Houthis fighting?

According to a February 2015 Newsweek report, **Houthis** are **fighting** "for things that all Yemenis crave: government accountability, the end to corruption, regular utilities, fair fuel prices, job opportunities for ordinary Yemenis and the end of Western influence.

The **Yemeni Civil War** is an ongoing conflict that began in 2015 between two factions: the Abdrabbuh Mansur Hadi led Yemeni government and the Houthi armed movement, along with their supporters and allies. Both claim to constitute the official government of Yemen.[533] Houthi forces currently controlling the capital Sanaʿa, allied with forces loyal to the former president Ali Abdullah Saleh, have clashed with the forces loyal to Hadi who are based in Aden. Al-Qaeda in the Arabian Peninsula (AQAP) and the Islamic State of Iraq and the Levant have also carried out attacks, with AQAP controlling swathes of territory in the hinterlands, and along stretches of the coast.[534] On 21 March 2015, after taking over Sanaʿa and the Yemeni government, the Houthi-led Supreme Revolutionary Committee declared a general mobilization to overthrow Hadi and expand their control by driving into southern provinces.[535] The Houthi offensive, allied with military forces loyal to Saleh, began fighting the next day in Lahij Governorate. By 25 March, Lahij fell to the Houthis and they reached the outskirts of Aden, the seat of power for Hadi's government.[536] Hadi fled the country the same day.[537] At the same time, a coalition led by Saudi Arabia launched military operations by using air strikes to restore the former Yemeni government.[538] The United States provided intelligence and logistical support for the

532 "John Kerry says Yemen's Houthis and Saudi coalition agree to ceasefire". *The Guardian*. 15 November 2016. Retrieved 17 November 2016.

533 Orkaby, Asher (25 March 2015). "Houthi Who?". Foreign Affairs. Archived from the original on 27 March 2015. Retrieved 25 March 2015.

534 "Yemen in Crisis". Council on Foreign Relations. 8 July 2015. Archivedfrom the original on 9 May 2015.

535 Abdul-Aziz Oudah. "Yemen observer". Archived from the original on 21 November 2015. Retrieved 18 November 2015.

536 "Yemen's president flees Aden as rebels close in". The Toronto Star. 25 March 2015. Archived from the original on 2 April 2015. Retrieved 25 March2015.

537 "Saudi Arabia: Yemen's President Hadi Arrives In Saudi Capital Riyadh". The Huffington Post. 26 March 2015. Archived from the original on 28 March 2015. Retrieved 26 March 2015.

538 Egypt, Jordan, Sudan and Pakistan ready for ground offensive in Yemen: report". the globe and mail. 26 March 2015. Archived from the original on 26 March 2015. Retrieved 26 March 2015.

campaign.[539] According to the UN and other sources, from March 2015 to December 2017, between 8,670–13,600 people were killed in Yemen, including more than 5,200 civilians, as well as estimates of more than 50,000 dead as a result of an ongoing famine due to the war.[540] The conflict has been widely seen as an extension of the Iran-Saudi Arabia proxy conflict and as a means to combat Iranian influence in the region.[541] In 2018, the United Nations warned that 13 million Yemeni civilians face starvation in what it says could become "the worst famine in the world in 100 years."[542] The international community has sharply condemned the Saudi Arabian-led bombing campaign, which has included widespread bombing of civilian areas.[543] The bombing campaign has killed or injured an estimated 17,729 civilians as of March 2019 according to the Yemen Data Project.[544] Despite this, the crisis has only recently begun to gain as much international media as the Syrian civil war.[545] The US has been providing bombs to aid the Saudi forces and airstrikes in Yemen. In March 2019, this has led the US senate to pass a resolution to end US support of Saudi Arabia.[546] It has

539 "Saudi Arabia Begins Air Assault in Yemen". The New York Times. 25 March 2015. Archived from the original on 26 March 2015. Retrieved 25 March 2015.

540 20 Killed in Saudi Airstrike in Yemen". Retrieved 31 December 2017.

Press, Associated. "50,000 children in Yemen have died of starvation and disease so far this year, monitoring group says". chicagotribune.com. Retrieved 2018-07-07.

541 Yemen crisis: Why is there a war? - BBC News

Who are the Houthis and why are they fighting the Saudi coalition in Yemen? | World news | The Guardian

542 "Yemen could be 'worst famine in 100 years'". BBC. 15 October 2018. Retrieved 15 October 2018.

543 Saudi Arabia and al-Qaeda Unite in Yemen Archived 10 February 2017 at the Wayback Machine, Huffington Post, "Despite the international community's condemnation of Saudi Arabia's bombing of civilian areas in Yemen, ... "

544 Raghavan, Sudarsan (27 March 2019). "Airstrike by Saudi-led coalition said to hit near Yemeni hospital, killing 8, including 5 children". The Washington Post. Retrieved 31 March 2019.

    1. ↑

545 Yemen: Faces of the world's forgotten war | World News | Sky News

https://www.amnesty.org/en/latest/news/2015/09/yemen-the-forgotten-war/

546   Gould, Joe (2019-03-14). "Senate passes resolution to end US support of Saudi Arabia in Yemen, 54-46". Defense News. Retrieved 2019-05-07.

since been vetoed by President of the United States Donald Trump, and in May, the Senate failed to override the veto.[547]

The Saudi- and United Arab Emirates-led coalition fighting in Yemen is under unprecedented pressure from the international community to end its involvement in the war after the killing of the Saudi journalist Jamal Khashoggi.

Since the coalition intervened in 2015, Yemen has become the worst humanitarian crisis in the world, according to the UN. Rights groups say up to 56,000 people have been killed, half of the 28 million-strong population are starving and the country is suffering the worst cholera epidemic in modern history.

But who are the coalition fighting, and why has the war descended into a stalemate? Yemen's Houthi rebels are a decades-old resistance movement, born in opposition to Saudi Arabia's religious influence. Although they cannot hold out forever against the coalition's air power and blockades, they say they are determined not to give up.

Origins as an anti-Saudi resistance group

The Houthi movement was founded in the 1990s by Hussein Badreddin al-Houthi, a member of Yemen's Zaidi Shia minority, which makes up about one-third of the population. Yemeni soldiers killed Hussein in 2004, and the group is now led by his brother Abdul Malik.

The Zaidis, once a powerful force in north Yemen, were sidelined during the 1962-70 civil war and then further alienated in the 1980s as Salafist Sunni ideals gained prominence across the border in Saudi Arabia, which exported the ideology to Yemen. In response, Zaidi clerics began to militarise their followers against Riyadh and its allies.

The intermittent insurgency gained support from Shia Yemenis fed up with the corruption and cruelty of the long-time authoritarian president and Saudi ally, Ali Abdullah Saleh, particularly during the aftermath of 9/11 and the US invasion of Iraq.

Role in the Arab spring

Popular protests and several assassination attempts forced Saleh to resign in 2012. The Houthis, as one of the only revolutionary groups with military experience, steadily gained control of territory outside their northern heartlands.

As they grew more powerful they pulled out of transition talks aimed at creating a new and stable Yemeni government after Saleh's downfall. In 2015 they allied with their former enemy Saleh, seizing the capital, Sana'a, and overthrowing the new president, Abd Rabbu Mansour Hadi.

---

547 Gould, Joe (2019-05-03). "Senate fails to override Trump veto on Yemen military assistance". *Defense News*. Retrieved 2019-05-07.

Goals in Yemen's civil war

The Houthis' slogan, known as the *sarkha*, or scream, is "God is great, death to America, death to Israel, curse on the Jews, victory to Islam." Apart from the resistance narrative, the Houthis have no stated political or governance goals for Yemen, despite the fact they are currently in control of both Sana'a and Hodeidah, a Red Sea port city through which 80% of the country's imports flow.

After they seized Sana'a in 2015, forcing Hadi to flee, the exiled Yemeni government asked its allies in Saudi Arabia and the UAE to launch a military campaign to drive out the Houthis.

Last December the Houthis turned on and killed Saleh after realising he was about to switch sides again to ally with the Saudi-led coalition. His death has further destabilised the chaotic Houthi command structure. Infighting is rife among Houthi leaders, military wings and clerics.

Throughout the war the Houthis have been accused of torturing and killing journalists and critics, siphoning off aid supplies, using civilian infrastructure as a shield for military activity and persecuting the country's Jewish and Baha'i minorities.

Relationship with Iran

The Houthis have variously said their tactics are modelled on those of the Viet Cong and resistance movements in Latin America as well as Lebanon's fearsome Shia Hezbollah, with which they have obvious kinship.

Both Hezbollah and Iran have increased their provision of guns, missiles, military training and funds for the Houthi war effort since 2014, happy to see their Saudi enemies expend soldiers and money on the Yemeni stalemate.

The extent of Tehran's influence over the Houthis' decision-making processes is unclear, however. The Houthis have acted expressly against Iran's advice on several occasions during the war, including a demand not to take over Sana'a in 2015.

Prospect of peace talks

Peace talks in Geneva in September this year – the first since 2016 – were cancelled after the Houthi delegation failed to arrive, citing security concerns. The UN is now working overtime to ensure the success of new talks, which are supposed to take place in Sweden by the end of November.

Several confidence-building measures are being implemented that were previously lacking, including the evacuation of wounded Houthi fighters to Oman and a security guarantee from Kuwait for travelling Houthi politicians. In turn, the Houthi leadership has said it will stop attacks on the Saudi-led coalition – their most significant concession in years, although there is still evidence of fighting.

The main issue will be the fate of Hodeidah, a significant source of revenue for the Houthis and arguably their most important asset. The UN wants both parties to agree to place it under UN jurisdiction, which it says is the only way to alleviate Yemen's cholera and malnutrition crises.

From other hand, The UK has put forward a UN security council resolution that calls for an immediate truce in the Yemeni port city of Hodeidah and guarantees of safe delivery of food and medicine.

The draft resolution is opposed by Saudi Arabia, which is leading airstrikes against Houthi rebels, and it is unclear how much effort the US is prepared to make to push it to a vote at the security council. A parallel peace effort being led by the UN also hangs in the balance as negotiations continue over safe passage of Houthi rebels to peace talks in Sweden.

On the same day the resolution was circulated among council members, Hodeidah residents reported the resumption of bombing by the Saudi-led coalition, ending a short lull in the battle for the city.

The resolution sets a two-week deadline for both Houthi rebels in control of Hodeidah and the Saudi-led coalition to remove all barriers to humanitarian aid, according to a copy seen by Agence France-Presse before a security council session on Monday.

The warring sides must "facilitate the unhindered flow of commercial and humanitarian food, water, fuel, medicine and other essential imports across the country" from Hodeidah, through which 80% of Yemen's imports flows, the text says.

It calls for a large injection of foreign currency into the country's economy through the central bank to support the collapsing Yemeni rial and for salaries of civil servants, teachers and health workers to be paid within one month. The resolution calls on the warring parties to cooperate with UN-brokered peace talks scheduled to begin later this month.

Imagine a navigation system in which you enter the following destination: 'Peace for Yemen'. It would lead you to the Bayan Palace in Kuwait, where peace talks have been underway since 21 April 2016. But it would also give you alternative routes to Riyadh, the EU, the US, Tehran and last but not least, to countless stakeholders in Yemen. Basically, the system would go berserk.

The conflict in Yemen, now in its second year, is not a struggle between two sides. There are no easily distinguishable good guys and bad guys. There is not one big war; there are many small wars between different groups with different agendas, with different regional and international backers. There is not one ceasefire that needs to hold, there are many ceasefires.

This is the reality that the Houthi/Saleh alliance and the Hadi government – the only official negotiating parties, with the UN as broker – are facing. Assuming they know what they want to get out of these negotiations (which is not at all certain), they cannot simply proceed; there are numerous players outside the palace, buzzing in their ears.

This applies most notably to the government headed by President Abd Rabbuh Mansour Hadi. It cannot make any concessions to the alliance of Houthi rebels and former president Ali Abdullah Saleh (hereafter referred to collectively as the Houthis) without the approval of the Saudi-led coalition that responded to Hadi's request to intervene and launch airstrikes on Houthi targets after rebel forces closed in on the president's southern stronghold of Aden in March 2015.

Saudi Arabia's buzzing should come as little surprise, given its involvement in the conflict. Yet surprise or not, it will evidently complicate matters if the parties at the negotiating table are not the only decision makers.

The Houthis do not have a similar regional prompter. Shia-ruled Iran's support for them has never been as clear or strong as that of the Sunni-ruled Saudis for Hadi, whatever Riyadh may tell the world about Tehran's sponsorship of the Houthis. However, they do not have unlimited room to maneuver either. They do not operate in a vacuum but in a country where loyalties are highly divided and where survival has become a daily struggle.

That, it seems, is the horse the UN is betting on when it comes to convincing the Houthis to stay at the negotiating table, from which both parties have already walked away several times. The reasoning: when people are starving, the Houthis are affected too.

It remains to be seen whether this strategy will actually work. As one of the 20 or so ambassadors to Yemen, who have gathered in Kuwait to throw their weight behind the peace process, said: "The Houthis do not seem to be very impressed by this. They are used to hardship."

That is at least a realistic observation. Less realistic seems to be the idea that is currently circulating among the diplomatic corps, of a roadmap to elections, with a transitional period led by a consensus government under Hadi. The Hadi part makes the plan particularly tricky, and possibly ill-fated.

From a diplomatic point of view, the idea is understandable. Western and Gulf Cooperation Council governments have always maintained that Hadi is Yemen's legitimate leader. Although this legitimacy is debatable, that does not seem to bother the diplomatic community much. It will, however, bother the Houthis, who will want Hadi out before agreeing to anything. They are not the only ones; most Yemenis have little or no confidence in Hadi's leadership.

Across the negotiating table will be concerns about another politician: Ali Abdullah Saleh. The Hadi side will want to ensure that if elections are held, Saleh – or one of his relatives – will not participate. Why? Because he may win, having gained increasing support among Yemenis for his anti-Saudi stance.

And these are just a handful of the issues. Among the many others are the economy, security, restoration funds, and the inclusion of all factions and groups in Yemen that have felt excluded from previous reconciliation attempts. It is hardly a matter of first things first; all have priority.

Then there is the rise of extremist groups such as Al-Qaeda in the Arabian Peninsula (AQAP) and Islamic State. So far, they are the conflict's big winners, restoring some sort of governance and basic services in war-torn areas in the south, not unlike the Houthis did in the north in September 2014. And as the Houthis did then, these groups are also gaining popular support.

Despite all the obstacles, the diplomats in Kuwait are cautiously optimistic. They point to the fact that both parties are still at the negotiating table which, in their opinion, means they want a solution. They are equally positive about the ceasefire, which is holding for the most part. They emphasise that it is now or never, at the same time calling for a sustainable deal, with little room for ambiguities that could cause problems in the future.

That means, once a framework agreement is reached, hundreds of pages of detailed text will need to be drafted, with each word potentially opening a new round of negotiations. Securing a deal amid this plethora of parties, interests and personalities will be nothing short of a miracle.

It is a miracle that many Yemenis on the other side of the Arabian Peninsula no longer believe in. As one of them put it: "Whatever deal they cobble together with the selected parties, too much blood has been spilled and too many people will seek vengeance. And for blood, justice will always find a way in Yemen." *The situation further deteriorated when the Houthis killed ex-president Ali Abdullah Saleh on December 4, 2017. Saleh had **officially** aligned with the Houthis in May 2015, helping the Houthis gain control over much of northern Yemen. But the alliance was shaky at best. In August, one of Saleh's top advisers was shot and **killed** following a confrontation with the Houthis. On December 2, Saleh publicly split from the Houthis, seeking a "new page" with the Saudi-led coalition. "I call upon the brothers in neighboring states and the alliance to stop their aggression, lift the siege, open the airports and allow food aid and the saving of the wounded and we will turn a new page by virtue of our neighborliness," he said. Two days later he was killed by Houthi rebels in a roadside ambush.*

*Iranian officials celebrated Saleh's death. Ali Akbar Salehi, a senior aide to Supreme Leader Ayatollah Khamenei said Saleh got what he deserved, **according** to the Middle East Institute. Senior advisor Ali Akbar Velayti commented on the Yemeni people's control over their own future. "Ali Abdullah Saleh was killed and United Arab Emirates and Saudi Arabia conspiracy was foiled by the people of Yemen. The people will determine their own fate and they will win like the people of Syria, Iraq and Lebanon,"*

Who are Yemen's allies?

Iran is widely accused of backing the Houthis, a Zaydi Shiite movement that has been fighting Yemen's Sunni-majority government since 2004. The Houthis took control of the Yemeni capital Sanaa (left) in September 2014 and continued on towards Aden, Yemen's largest city. In response to Houthi advances, Saudi Arabia and other Arab states launched a military campaign in March 2015. Yemeni officials and Sunni states, most notably Saudi Arabia, have repeatedly alleged that Iran and its proxy Hezbollah have provided arms, training, and financial support to the Houthis. But Iranian and Hezbollah officials have denied or downplayed the claims.

Yemen desires to join the 24-year-old Gulf Cooperation Council (GCC), a sub-regional organization which groups Saudi Arabia, Kuwait, Bahrain, Qatar, the United Arab Emirates, and Oman in an economic and security alliance.

What does houthis mean?

Houthi movement. ... Houthi slogan reading "God is Greater, Death to America, Death to Israel, Curse on the Jews, Victory to Islam" The Houthis are a large clan originating from Yemen's northwestern Saada province. They practice the Zaydi form of Shiism. Zaydis make up around 35 percent of Yemen's population. A Zaydi imamate ruled Yemen for 1,000 years, before being overthrown in 1962. Since then, the Zaydis – stripped of their political power – have struggled to restore their authority and influence in Yemen. In the 1980s, the Houthi clan began a movement to revive Zaydi traditions, feeling threatened by state-funded Salafist preachers who established a base in Houthi areas. Not all Zaydis, however, align with the Houthi movement. Houthi insurgents have clashed with Yemen's government for more than a decade. Since 2011, the Houthi movement has expanded beyond its Zaydi roots and become a wider movement opposed to President Abd Rabbuh Mansour Hadi. The insurgents have also begun referring to themselves as Ansarullah, or "Party of God." As to the **Zaydism' comparision on the type of Shiism practiced in Iran** Like other Shiites, Zaydis believe that only descendants of the Prophet Mohammed's

cousin and son-in-law, Ali, have the right to lead the Muslim community as imams -

divinely-appointed successors of the Prophet. Most adherents of Zaydism reside in

Yemen, and Zaydis make up around eight percent of the world's 70 million Shiites.

But the Zaydis are distinct from the "Twelver" form of Shiism practiced by the

majority of the world's Shiites, including most Shiites in Iran. Twelver Shiites believe

the twelfth imam, whom they consider infallible, disappeared in 874AD and will one

day return to usher in an age of justice as the Mahdi, or promised one. In the Mahdi's

absence, Twelver Shiites believe clerics can substitute for his authority on certain

issues. The faithful are obliged to obey the clerics' religious rulings, a power

transferred to Iran's theocracy after the 1979 revolution. Zaydis, also known

as "Fivers," believe that Zayd, the great-grandson of Ali, was the rightful fifth imam.

But Twelver Shiites consider Zayd's brother, Mohammad al Baqir, the fifth imam.

The Zaydis do not recognize the later Twelver imams, and instead believe anyone related to Ali is eligible to lead the Muslim community. They also reject the Twelver doctrine that the imam is infallible.

As to the question How Houthis are now supported ? Iranian officials have supported the Houthis' cause and compared the group to Hezbollah. "Iran supports the rightful struggles of Ansarullah in Yemen and considers this movement as part of the successful Islamic Awakening movements," Ali Akbar Velayati, senior advisor to Supreme Leader Ayatollah Ali Khamenei, said in October 2014. But Tehran has repeatedly denied providing arms, funds or training to the Houthis.

What do the Houthis believe?

Zaydis believe he was a model of a pure caliph who should have ruled instead of the Umayyads. The Houthis have made fighting corruption the centerpiece of their political program, at least nominally. The distinguishing feature of Zayd's remembered biography is that he fought against a corrupt regime

The Houthi insurgency in Yemen

The Houthi insurgency in Yemen,[548] also known as the Houthi rebellion, Sa'dah War, or Sa'dah conflict, was a military rebellion pitting Zaidi Shia Houthis (though the movement also includes Sunnis[549]) against the Yemeni military that began in Northern Yemen and has since escalated into a full-scale civil war. The conflict was sparked in 2004 by the government's attempt to arrest Hussein Badreddin al-Houthi, a Zaidi religious leader of the Houthis and a former parliamentarian on whose head the government had placed a $55,000 bounty.[550] Initially, most of the fighting took place

---

548 Hill, Ginny (2007-02-05). "Yemen fears return of insurgency". BBC News. Archived from the original on 2008-04-06. Retrieved 2008-05-23.

McGregor, Andrew (August 12, 2004). "Shi'ite Insurgency in Yemen: Iranian Intervention or Mountain Revolt?" (PDF). Terrorism Monitor. The Jamestown Foundation. 2 (16): 4–6. Archived from the original (PDF) on November 21, 2006. Retrieved 2008-05-23.

549 Debunking Media Myths About the Houthis in War-Torn Yemen · Global Voices". 1 April 2015. Archived from the original on 1 September 2017. Retrieved 11 September 2017.

550 Profile: Yemen's Houthi fighters". Al Jazeera. 2009-07-12. Archived from the original on 2009-12-22. Retrieved 2009-12-22

in Sa'dah Governorate in northwestern Yemen, but some of the fighting spread to neighbouring governorates Hajjah, 'Amran, al-Jawf and the Saudi province of Jizan. Since 2014 the nature of the insurgency has changed with the Houthi takeover in Yemen and then into the ongoing Yemeni civil war (2015–present) with a major Saudi-led intervention in Yemen beginning in 2015.[551]

General Ali Mohsen al-Ahmar commanded the Yemeni security forces during the conflict and led all the government offensives from 2004 until 2011, when he resigned his post to defend protesters during the Yemeni Revolution.[552]

A Houthi power grab in Sana'a escalated on 20 January 2015, when the rebels attacked the president's residence and swept into the presidential palace. President Abed Rabbo Mansour Hadi was inside the residence as it came under "heavy shelling" for half an hour, but he was unharmed and protected by guards, according to Information Minister Nadia Al-Sakkaf. Presidential guards surrendered the residence after being assured that Hadi could safely evacuate. The U.N. Security Council called an emergency meeting about the unfolding events. United Nations Secretary-General Ban Ki Moon expressed concern over the "deteriorating situation" in Yemen and urged all sides to cease hostilities.[553] On 22 January, President Abed Rabbo Mansour Hadi and Prime Minister Khaled Bahah tendered their resignations to parliament, which reportedly refused to accept them.[554]

In 1962, a revolution in North Yemen ended over 1,000 years of rule by Zaidi Imams, who claimed descent from the Hashemites. Sa'dah, in the north, was their main stronghold and since their fall from power the region was largely ignored economically and remains underdeveloped. The Yemeni government has little authority in Sa'dah.[555]

During Yemen's 1994 civil war, the Wahhabis, an Islamic group adhering to a strict version of Sunni Islam found in neighboring Saudi Arabia, helped the government in its fight against the secessionist south. Zaidis complain the government has subsequently allowed the Wahhabis too strong a voice in Yemen. Saudi Arabia, for its

551 Crises multiply for divided Yemen". BBC News. Archived from the original on 23 October 2014. Retrieved 17 October 2014.

552 he crucible of Yemen". Al Jazeera. 22 May 2011. Archived from the original on 25 October 2011. Retrieved 17 October 2014.

553 *Rebels capture Yemen presidential palace, shell residence". USA today. 20 January 2015. Archived from the original on 20 January 2015. Retrieved 20 January 2015.*

"Yemen rebels overtake presidential palace". Al Jazeera. 20 January 2015. Archived from the original on 20 January 2015. Retrieved 20 January 2015.

554 Yemen crisis: President resigns as rebels tighten hold". BBC. January 22, 2015. Archived from the original on August 20, 2018. Retrieved January 22,2015.

555 Profile: Yemen's Houthi fighters". Al Jazeera. 2009-07-12. Archived from the original on 2009-12-22. Retrieved 2009-12-22

part, worries that strife instigated by the Zaidi sect so close to Yemen's border with Saudi Arabia could stir up groups in Saudi Arabia itself.[556]

The conflict was sparked in 2004 by the government's attempt to arrest Hussein Badreddin al-Houthi, a Zaidi religious leader of the Houthis and a former parliamentarian on whose head the government had placed a $55,000 bounty.[557]

Hussein Badreddin al-Houthi movement accused Ali Abdullah Saleh of massive financial corruption and criticized him for being backed by Saudi Arabia and United States[558]at the expense of the Yemeni people[559] and Yemen's sovereignty.[560]

Objectives

When armed conflict for the first time erupted in 2004 between the Yemeni government and Houthis, the then Yemeni president accused Houthis and other Islamic opposition parties of trying to overthrow the government and the republican system. The Yemeni government alleged that the Houthis were seeking to overthrow it and to implement Zaidi religious law.

Houthi leaders for their part rejected the accusation by saying that they had never rejected the president or the republican system but were only defending themselves against government attacks on their community.[561] The Houthis said that they were "defending their community against discrimination" and government aggression.[562] The Yemeni government has accused Iran of directing and financing the insurgency.

According to a February 2015 *Newsweek* report, Houthis are fighting "for things that all Yemenis crave: government accountability, the end to corruption, regular utilities, fair fuel prices, job opportunities for ordinary Yemenis and the end of Western influence."[563]

556 Profile: Yemen's Houthi fighters". Al Jazeera. 2009-07-12. Archived from the original on 2009-12-22. Retrieved 2009-12-22

557 Profile: Yemen's Houthi fighters". Al Jazeera. 2009-07-12. Archived from the original on 2009-12-22. Retrieved 2009-12-22.

558 Riedel, Bruce (2017-12-18). "Who are the Houthis, and why are we at war with them?". *Brookings Institution*. Archived from the original on 2018-06-12. Retrieved 2018-06-12.

559 Yemeni forces kill rebel cleric". *BBC News*. 10 September 2004. Archived from the original on 21 November 2006.

560 Streuly, Dick (2015-02-12). "5 Things to Know About the Houthis of Yemen". *WSJ*. Archived from the original on 2018-06-12. Retrieved 2018-07-04.

561 Arrabyee, Nasser (2005-05-25). "Rebellion continues". *Al-Ahram Weekly*. Archived from the original on 2007-06-19. Retrieved 2007-04-11.
Deadly blast strikes Yemen mosque". BBC News. 2008-05-02. Archived from the original on 2008-05-05. Retrieved 2008-05-23.

562 Johnsen, Gregory D. (February 20, 2007). "Yemen Accuses Iran of Meddling in its Internal Affairs" (PDF). *Terrorism Focus*. **4** (2): 3–4. Archived from the original (PDF) on June 16, 2007. Retrieved 2007-04-07.

563 "Photo Essay: The Rise of the Houthis". *Newsweek*. 9 February 2015. Archived from the original on 12 February 2015. Retrieved 17 February2015.

In an interview with the *Yemen Times*, Hussein Al-Bukhari, a Houthi insider, said that the Houthis' preferred political system is a republic with elections where women can also hold political positions, and that they do not seek to form a cleric-led government after the model of the Islamic Republic of Iran for "we cannot apply this system in Yemen because the followers of the Shafi doctrine are bigger in number than the Zaydis."[564]

Phase 1: June–September 2004

From June to August 2004, government troops battled supporters of al-Houthi in the north.[565] Estimates of the dead range from 500 to 1,000.[566] On 10 September, Yemeni forces killed al-Houthi.[567] Since then, the rebellion has been led by one of his brothers, Abdul-Malik al-Houthi,[568] while his father, Badr Eddin al-Houthi, became the group's spiritual leader.[569]

Phase 2: March–June 2005

Between March and April 2005, some 1,500 people were killed in a resurgence of fighting between government forces and supporters of the slain cleric, now calling themselves Houthis.[570]

In May 2005, the rebels rejected an offer of a presidential pardon by President Ali Abdullah Saleh after their conditions for surrender were refused by the government and minor clashes continued. On May 21, the government released estimates of the impact of the insurgency, announcing that it was responsible for 552 deaths, 2,708 injures, and over US$ 270 million in economic damages.[571]

---

564 Al-Bukhari to the Yemen Times: "The Houthis' takeover can not be called an invasion"". *Yemen Times*. 21 October 2014. Archived from the original on 17 February 2015. Retrieved 17 February 2015.

565 Clashes 'leave 118 dead' in Yemen". BBC News. 2004-07-03. Archivedfrom the original on 2007-01-06. Retrieved 2007-02-03.

566 Armed Conflicts Report - Yemen". Ploughshares.ca. Archived from the original on 2009-10-30. Retrieved 2009-11-09.

567 Yemeni forces kill rebel cleric". BBC News. 2004-09-10. Archived from the original on 2006-11-21. Retrieved 2007-01-30.

568 Arrabyee, Nasser (2005-05-25). "Rebellion continues". *Al-Ahram Weekly*. Archived from the original on 2007-06-19. Retrieved 2007-04-11.

569 al-Shabab al-Mum'en / Shabab al-Moumineen (Believing Youth)". GlobalSecurity.org. Archived from the original on 11 April 2010. Retrieved 29 December 2009.

570 Armed Conflicts Report - Yemen". Ploughshares.ca. Archived from the original on 2009-10-30. Retrieved 2009-11-09.

571 Arrabyee, Nasser (2005-05-25). "Rebellion continues". *Al-Ahram Weekly*. Archived from the original on 2007-06-19. Retrieved 2007-04-11.
al-Shabab al-Mum'en / Shabab al-Moumineen (Believing Youth)".
GlobalSecurity.org. Archived from the original on 11 April 2010. Retrieved 29 December 2009.

On 23 June 2005, the Houthis' military commander Abdullah al-Ruzami surrendered to Yemeni authorities after tribal mediators worked out a deal with the government.[572]

Phase 3: November 2005 – 2006

Fighting broke out in November 2005 and continued until early 2006. The pro-government Hamdan tribe, led by Sheikh Abdullah al-Awjari, battled with pro-Houthi tribes and Houthis tried to assassinate a Ministry of Justice official in Dhamar The fighting ended before the presidential elections that year[573] and in March 2006, the Yemeni government freed more than 600 captured Shī'a fighters.[574] There was no data with regards to casualties in 2006, but they were said to be significantly lower than those of the previous year.[575]

Phase 4: January–June 2007

Fighting broke out on 28 January 2007, when militants attacked a number of government installations, killing six soldiers and injuring 20 more.[576]

Further attacks on 31 January left six more soldiers dead and 10 wounded.[577] A further ten soldiers died and 20 were wounded in an attack on an army roadblock near the Saudi Arabian border on 1 February.[578] Though there was no official confirmation of militant casualties in the attacks, government sources claim three rebel fighters were killed in a security operation following the 31 January attacks[579]

In February, the government launched a major offensive against the rebels involving 30,000 troops.[580] By 19 February, almost 200 members of the security forces and over

572

573 Christopher Boucek; Marina Ottaway (2010). *Yemen on the Brink*. Carnegie Endowment for International Peace. ISBN 9780870033292. Retrieved 17 October 2014.

574 "Yemen tells Shi'ite rebels to disband or face war". Reuters. 2004-01-29. Archived from the original on 2007-02-06. Retrieved 2007-01-30.

575 Armed Conflicts Report - Yemen". Ploughshares.ca. Archived from the original on 2009-10-30. Retrieved 2009-11-09.

576 *'Shia gunmen' kill Yemeni troops". BBC News. 2004-01-28. Archivedfrom the original on 2007-02-04. Retrieved 2007-01-30.*

Al-Mahdi, Khaled (2007-02-15). "95 Killed in Yemen Clashes". ArabNews. Archived from the original on 2007-09-30. Retrieved 2007-04-11.

577 "Shi'ite rebels kill six Yemen soldiers - Web site". Reuters. 2007-02-01. Archived from the original on 2009-06-18. Retrieved 2007-02-03.

578 "Yemeni soldiers killed in attack". Al Jazeera English. 2007-02-01. Archived from the original on 2007-02-03. Retrieved 2007-02-02.

579 "10 soldiers killed in attack in Yemen". Middle East Online. 2007-02-02. Archived from the original on 2007-09-28. Retrieved 2007-02-03

580 *Arrabyee, Nasser (2007-04-04). "Yemen's rebels undefeated". Al-Ahram Weekly. Archived from the original on 2007-04-16. Retrieved 2007-04-11.*

100 rebels had died in the fighting.[581] A further 160 rebels were killed in the subsequent two weeks.[582] A French student was also killed.[583]

A ceasefire agreement was reached on 16 June 2007. The rebel leaders agreed to lay down arms and go into exile in Qatar (by whom the agreement had been mediated), while the government agreed to release rebel prisoners, help pay for reconstruction and assist with IDPs returning home.[584] In total some 1,500 people were killed by the conflict in 2007, including 800 government troops, 600 rebels and 100 civilians.[585]

Phase 5: March–July 2008

Armed incidents resumed in April 2008, when seven Yemeni soldiers died in a rebel ambush on 29 April.[586] On 2 May, 15 worshippers were killed and 55 wounded in a bombing at the Bin Salman Mosque in Sa'dah as crowds of people left Friday prayers. The government blamed the rebels for the bombing, but the Houthis denied responsibility.[587] Shortly after the attack, three soldiers and four rebels died in overnight skirmishes.[588]

On 12 May, clashes between Yemeni soldiers and rebels near the border with Saudi Arabia killed 13 soldiers and 26 rebels.[589] During fighting in May 2008, a total of 1,000 government forces were killed and 3,000 injured. Some 70,000 people were

---

581 "More than 100 killed in 5 days of clashes between army and Shiite rebels clashes in Yemen, officials say". *International Herald Tribune*. 2007-02-19. Archived from the original on 2007-04-01. Retrieved 2007-04-11.

582 "160 rebels killed in Yemen". *Israel Herald*. 2007-03-07. Archived from the original on 2007-09-28. Retrieved 2007-04-11.

583 "Two killed in Yemen attack including a Frenchman". Reuters. 26 March 2007. Archived from the original on 22 January 2010. Retrieved 29 December 2009.

584 Al-Hajj, Ahmed (2007-06-17). "Yemen's government, Shiite rebels negotiate end to 3-year conflict". *The Seattle Times*. Archived from the original on 2007-06-20. Retrieved 2007-06-17.

585 Armed Conflicts Report - Yemen". Ploughshares.ca.

586 "Dozens of casualties in Yemen mosque blast". *France 24*. Reuters. 2008-05-02. Archived from the original on 2009-06-18. Retrieved 2008-05-23

587 "Deaths in Yemeni mosque blast". Al Jazeera English. 2008-05-02. Archived from the original on 2008-05-05. Retrieved 2008-05-23.
"Deadly blast strikes Yemen mosque". BBC News. 2008-05-02. Archived from the original on 2008-05-05. Retrieved 2008-05-23.

588 "7 die as Yemeni troops, rebels clash after mosque attack". *The Jerusalem Post*. Associated Press. 2008-05-03. Archived from the original on 2011-07-13. Retrieved 2008-05-23.

589 "Heavy clashes break out between Yemeni soldiers and Shiite rebels in nor". *International Herald Tribune*. Associated Press. 2008-05-12. Retrieved 2008-05-23.

displaced by the fighting.[590] President Saleh declared an end to fighting in the northern Sa'dah governorate on 17 July 2008.[591]

Phase 6: Operation Scorched Earth, August 2009 – February 2010

On 11 August 2009, the government promised to use an "iron fist" against the rebels. The Yemeni troops, backed by tanks and fighter aircraft, launched a fresh offensive, code-named Operation Scorched Earth,[592] against the Houthis in the northern Sa'ada province. Hundreds of thousands of people were displaced by the fighting.

On 17 September, more than 80 people were killed in an air raid on a camp for displaced people in northern Yemen.[593]

The conflict took on an international dimension late in the month. Clashes were reported between the Houthis and Saudi security forces near the border.[594] Also, Yemeni officials captured a boat in the Red Sea that was transporting anti-tank shells and, according to some reports, five Iranian "instructors" sent to help the Houthis.[595] Various official Iranian sources responded, calling this claim a politically motivated fabrication, and stating that the ship was traveling for business activities carrying no consignment.[596] In early November the rebels stated that Saudi Arabia was permitting Yemeni army units to launch attacks from across the border at a base in Jabal al-Dukhan, charges which were denied by the Yemeni government.[597] In late October, heavy clashes in the area of Razih led to the Houthis capturing two military headquarters and killing Yemeni General Amr Ali Mousa Al-Uuzali.[598] In early

---

590 Armed Conflicts Report - Yemen". Ploughshares.ca. Archived from the original on 2009-10-30. Retrieved 2009-11-09.

591 Yemen: Hundreds Unlawfully Arrested in Rebel Conflict". Human Rights Watch. 2008-10-24. Archived from the original on 2010-08-26. Retrieved 2009-11-09.

592 "Yemen denies warplane shot down". Al Jazeera English. 2009-10-02. Archived from the original on 2009-10-15. Retrieved 2009-11-09.

593 "'Many killed' in Yemen air raid". BBC News. 2009-09-17. Archived from the original on 2009-09-30. Retrieved 2009-11-09.

594 "Yemen rebels 'seize Saudi area'". BBC News. 2009-11-04. Archivedfrom the original on 2009-11-07. Retrieved 2009-11-09.

595 "Yemenis intercept 'Iranian ship'". BBC News. 2009-10-27. Archivedfrom the original on 2009-10-30. Retrieved 2009-11-02

596 "Iran says documents prove Yemen ship had no arms". Press TV. 2009-10-28. Archived from the original on 2012-10-05. Retrieved 2009-11-02.

597 "Yemen rebels accuse Saudi". France 24. Agence France-Presse. 2009-11-02. Archived from the original on 2011-07-11. Retrieved 2009-11-02

598 "Houthis kill top Yemeni commander". Presstv.com. 2009-10-25. Archived from the original on 2011-07-15. Retrieved 2009-11-09.

November, General Ali Salem al-Ameri and regional security chief Ahmed Bawazeir were killed in a Houthi ambush as they were returning from Saudi Arabia[599]

Attacking Saudi Arabian Borders, 4 November 2009

The conflict took on an international dimension on 4 November 2009 when the Houthis attacked the Saudi border, killed one of the Saudi border guards, seized Al Khubah Village and other villages.[600] The Houthis accuse Saudi Arabia of supporting the Yemeni government in attacks against them. It was not clear what type of support they meant. The Saudi government denied this.[601] The rebels shot dead a Saudi security officer in a cross-border attack. The rebels took control of a mountainous section inside Saudi Arabia, in the border region of Jabal al-Dukhan[602]and occupied two villages inside Saudi territory.[603] The houthis had entered Saudi territory and attacked patrols, and that a second soldier later died from wounds sustained in the same clash.[604] On 5 November, Saudi Arabia responded by launching heavy air strikes on rebels in northern Yemen, and moved troops nearer the border. Saudi government officials said only that the air force had bombed Yemeni rebels who had seized a border area inside the kingdom, which they said had now been recaptured. The officials said at least 40 rebels had been killed in the fighting. The Saudi government adviser said no decision had yet been taken to send troops across the border, but made clear Riyadh was no longer prepared to tolerate the Yemeni rebels.[605] The Saudi assault continued the following day, as Saudi residents near the southern border of Jizan Province were evacuated.[606] At the same time, a Houthi spokesman reported

---

599 Ambush kills 3 Yemeni soldiers, 2 top officers". PressTV. 3 November 2009. Archived from the original on 24 December 2014.

600 Timeline: Yemen". BBC News. 2009-11-11. Archived from the original on 2011-02-08. Retrieved 2009-12-22.

601 Timeline: Yemen". BBC News. 2009-11-11. Archived from the original on 2011-02-08. Retrieved 2009-12-22.

602 Yemen rebels 'seize Saudi area'". BBC News. 2009-11-04. Archivedfrom the original on 2009-11-07. Retrieved 2009-11-09.

603 "Riyadh continues air raids on northern Yemen". Press TV. 24 December 2009. Archived from the original on 8 October 2012. Retrieved 29 December2009.

1. ^ "Houthis Say they Will Withdraw from Saudi if Riyadh Ends Attacks". Naharnet (AFP). 23 December 2009. Retrieved 29 December 2009.

604 Saudi air force hits Yemen rebels after border raid". Swissinfo.ch. 2009-11-05. Archived from the original on 2012-09-11. Retrieved 2009-11-09.

Hilder, James. "Yemen civil war spills over border as Saudi official is killed in attack". Archived from the original on June 29, 2011. Retrieved November 5, 2009.

605 "Saudi air force hits Yemen rebels after border raid". Swissinfo.ch. 2009-11-05. Archived from the original on 2012-09-11. Retrieved 2009-11-09.

to the media that they had captured Saudi troops.[607] On 16 November, Yemen forces killed two Houthi commanders, Abbas Aaida and Abu Haider. On 19 November, Yemeni forces took control of al-Malaheez, killing the local commander Ali al-Qatwani.[608]

Houthi leaders claim that United States involvement in the war started on 14 December 2009 when the US launched 28 air raids.[609] At least 120 people were killed and 44 injured by the alleged US air raids on the regions of Amran, Hajjah and Sa'dah in northern Yemen. Houthis claimed air raids on 18 December killed 63 civilians, including 28 children and injured at least 90 people[610]U.S. President Barack Obama claimed he had authorised the strikes against al-Qaeda.[611] On 20 December, Saudi air strike killed some civilians. According to a spokesman for the Houthis, a Saudi attack killed 54 people in the town of Al Nadheer in the northern province of Sa'dah. The group also claimed that Saudi forces were advancing on the nearby town of Zawa, also in Sa'dah, and had fired more than 200 shells.[612]

On 22 December, the Houthis stated that they managed to repulse Saudi Arabian forces trying to infiltrate into the province of Sa'dah, killing an unspecified number of Saudi soldiers in a battle in the border region.[613]

The fighting between Yemeni and Saudi forces and Houthis killed at least 119 Yemeni government forces, 263 Houthis, 277 civilians and 7 foreign civilians[614]Saudi casualties were confirmed at 82 at the time.[615] With more soldiers killed in

606 "Saudi forces keep up Houthi assault". Al Jazeera. 2009-11-06. Archivedfrom the original on 2009-11-09. Retrieved 2009-11-06.

607 Ersan, Inal (2009-11-06). "Yemeni rebels say capture Saudi soldiers: report". Reuters. Retrieved 2009-11-06.

608 "Saudi soldier, Houthi leaders killed in north Yemen". Press TV. 19 November 2009. Archived from the original on 15 July 2011. Retrieved 29 December 2009.

609 US fighter jets attack Yemeni fighters". Press TV. 14 December 2009. Archived from the original on 2 January 2010. Retrieved 29 December 2009

610 "US air raids kill 63 civilians in Yemen". Press TV. 18 December 2009. Archived from the original on 2016-01-19. Retrieved 29 December 2009.

611 Ross, Brian; Richard Esposito; Matthew Cole; Luis Martinez; Kirit Radia. "Obama Ordered U.S. Military Strike on Yemen Terrorists". ABC News. Archived from the original on 24 December 2009. Retrieved 29 December2009.

612 Liam Stack (21 December 2009). "Saudi air strike kills Yemen rebels as US drawn into fight". The Christian Science Monitor. Archived from the original on 19 September 2014. Retrieved 17 October 2014.

613 Houthis repel Saudi incursion into northern Yemen". Press TV. 23 December 2009. Archived from the original on 24 December 2009. Retrieved 23 December 2009.

614 Armed Conflicts Report - Yemen". Ploughshares.ca. Archived from the original on 2009-10-30. Retrieved 2009-11-09

subsequent clashes and missing soldiers being found dead, however, the casualties rose to 133 killed by 22 January 2010. The number of missing was put at six.[616]

In early January 2010, the Houthis chose the Iraqi cleric Grand Ayatollah Ali al-Sistani to mediate in their political standoff with the Yemeni government and to find a solution to the conflict. This choice was criticized by Saudi cleric Mohammad al-Arifi, a preacher at Riyadh's central mosque, who dismissed al-Sistani as "an infidel and debauched." The remarks by the Saudi cleric were considered extremely insulting by Shi'as around the world, causing major outrage in some Shi'a dominant countries like Iraq, Iran and Lebanon.[617]

On 13 January 2010, Operation Blow to the Head was launched in an attempt by the government to capture the city of Sa'adah. Security forces claimed they killed 34 and arrested at least 25 Houthis, as well as killing al-Qaeda in Yemen leader Abdullah al-Mehdar in the next two weeks of fighting.[618]

On 25 January 2010, the Houthis offered a truce.[619] Houthi leader Abdul Malek al-Houthi said they would stop fighting to prevent further civilian casualties and the withdrawal was a gesture for peace,[620] but warned that if the Saudis were to continue fighting the Houthis would go over into open warfare. A Saudi general announced that the Houthis had stopped fighting and were not on Saudi land anymore and that in response the Saudis also stopped fighting saying, "The battle has ended by God's will." But the Saudi king denied the Houthis had withdrawn saying they were forced out, and declared military victory for the end of their conflict with the Houthis[621] There have however been allegations that the Saudis launched new air raids on 29 January, thus breaking the truce.[622]

615 "Saudi Arabia says soldiers killed in Yemen". Press TV. 12 January 2010. Archived from the original on 2016-01-19. Retrieved 2010-01-12

616 Saudi: Bodies of 20 soldiers found on Yemen border Archived 2011-06-04 at the Wayback Machine, 23 January 2010.

617 "Salafis irate over ban on preacher". The National. Archived from the original on 11 October 2014. Retrieved 17 October 2014.

Sunni scholars against insulting Sistani Archived July 17, 2011, at the Wayback Machine

618 "Leader of Al Qaeda in Yemen 'killed in gun battle'". Daily Mail. London. 2010-01-13. Archived from the original on 2011-03-25. Retrieved 2010-12-26.

619 Houthis initiate truce with Saudi Arabia". Press TV. 25 January 2010. Archived from the original on 2011-07-15. Retrieved 2010-01-29.
"Saudis claim victory over Houthis". Press TV. 27 January 2010. Archived from the original on 2016-01-19. Retrieved 2010-01-29.

620

621 "Saudi-Houthi border fighting ends". Al Jazeera English. Archived from the original on 29 June 2011. Retrieved 17 October 2014.

622 "Despite truce call, Saudis pound northern Yemen". Press TV. 29 January 2010. Archived from the original on 2016-01-19. Retrieved 2010-01-29.

On 1 January the Yemeni government offered a conditional cease-fire. The cease-fire had five conditions which were the re-establishment of safe passage on roads, the surrender of mountain strongholds, a full withdrawal from all local authority property, the return of all military and public equipment seized during hostilities and the release of all the detained civilians and soldiers. On 30 January, Abdel-Malek al-Houthi released a video wherein he blamed the government for the recent round of fighting but said that: "Nevertheless, and for the fourth time, I announce our acceptance of the [government's] five conditions [for an end to the conflict] after the aggression stops ... the ball is now in the other party's court."[623] After the truce was accepted on 30 January, however, there were still some clashes between the Houthis and both Saudi and Yemeni forces.[624] Therefore, on 31 January the Yemeni government rejected the truce and launched a new round of attacks, killing 24 people.[625]

2010 conflict with pro-government tribes

In April, Houthi spokesman Mohammed Abdulsalam declared that rebels had captured the Manaba district in Sa'dah, with little government resistance. Government troops declared they had killed 30 Houthis who had tried to penetrate into Harf Sufyan District.

On July 17, 2010, the Houthis warned on their website that the government was preparing for another offensive against the Houthis. They said the government had been digging trenches from the Sana'a to Sa'ada. They claimed the army was trying to amass servicemen in villages and that soldiers in Amshia Bsfian region were creating an army stronghold on Mount Guide. The report came as the Yemeni government blamed Houthi fighters for recent ethnic clashes which had killed 11 people, including two soldiers, and for the kidnapping of two people in a market. The Houthis have denied these allegations and have claimed that it was the work of the government.[626]

On July 20, 2010, clashes broke out between Houthis and members of an army-backed tribe, led by Sheikh Sagheer Aziz, in the region of Souffian. A Houthi commander declared that the clashes had broken out because of Yemeni Army attacks on Houthis and local pro-Houthi tribes. Forty-nine people were reported killed in the clashes, including 20 tribal and 10 Houthi fighters. The Houthis also managed to surround the Yemeni military bases in the region.[627] Over the following days the Yemeni army and pro-government Bin Aziz tribes continued to clash with the Houthis. The government claimed that in the following two days, 20 fighters were killed on each side. A Houthi spokesman denied these claims, stating only three

---

623 Al Jazeera Yemen rebels renew ceasefire offer Archived 2010-01-31 at the Wayback Machine, January 30, 2010.

624 Press TV Saudis 'launch 17 air raids' on Houthis Archived 2011-07-15 at the Wayback Machine, 30 January 2010.

625 Press TV Yemen rejects Houthis' 4th peace offer Archived 2011-07-15 at the Wayback Machine, 31 January 2009.

626 Press TV 'Yemen preparing to attack Houthis' Archived 2011-07-15 at the Wayback Machine, 18 July 2010.

627 Press TV Fresh clashes claim 49 in north Yemen Archived 2010-08-12 at the Wayback Machine, 21 July 2010.

Houthi fighters had been killed in the clashes. Both sides have blamed each other for starting the clashes.[628] The UN expressed great concern about the situation in North Yemen.[629]

On July 23, Houthi spokesman Vayf-Allah al-Shami said calm had returned to the region and that a government committee was trying to mediate a cease-fire between the Houthis and the Bin Aziz tribes in the Souffian region.[630]

On July 27, Houthis seized a military post at al-Zaala in Harf Sufyan, capturing 200 soldiers of the army's Republican Guard. Tribal sources claimed they had inflicted 200 fatalities on the Houthis in al-Amsheya while suffering only 30 dead themselves. Houthi spokesman Abdul Salam denied the high number of killed and said the claims were highly exaggerated. Houthis said they recovered the bodies of 17 of their fighters, including that of rebel commander Abu Haidar, near the house of Sheikh Saghir Aziz in Al-Maqam, near Al-Zaala.[631]

On July 29, the Houthis released the 200 soldiers they had captured as a goodwill gesture. In total some 70 people had died since the clashes started.[632]

On November 22, one soldier was killed and two wounded in a roadside bombing. The next day 23 Houthi fighters and supporters were killed and 30 injured by a car bomb targeting a Shi'a religious procession in al-Jawf province.[633] On November 26, two Shi'a mourners were killed and eight injured by a bomb while on their way to Sa'adah city to attend Badreddin al-Houthi's funeral.[634]

In total, between 195 and 281 people were killed during this round violence, with the majority of the casualties on the Houthi side.[635]

---

628 Press TV More people killed in N Yemen clashes Archived 2010-08-12 at the Wayback Machine, 22 July 2010.

629 Press TV UN concerned about Yemen situation Archived 2010-08-12 at the Wayback Machine, 24 July 2010

630 Press TV Calm to return to north Yemen Archived 2010-08-12 at the Wayback Machine, 23 July 2010.

631 Google News Yemen Shiite rebels capture 200 soldiers: military officialArchived 2011-03-03 at the Wayback Machine, 27 July 2010.

632 Press TV Houthis release 200 Yemeni soldiers Archived 2010-08-12 at the Wayback Machine, 29 July 2010.

633 "Car bomb kills 23 in northern Yemen". Press TV. 24 November 2010. Archived from the original on 19 January 2011. Retrieved 26 December2010.

"Bomb kills Shia mourners in N Yemen". Press TV. 26 November 2010. Archived from the original on 11 January 2011. Retrieved 26 December2010.

634 "Bomb kills Shia mourners in N Yemen". Press TV. 26 November 2010. Archived from the original on 11 January 2011. Retrieved 26 December2010.

635 "Yemen (2004 – first combat deaths)". Ploughshares.ca. Archived from the original on 23 March 2012. Retrieved 17 October 2014.

2011 Yemeni Revolution

A major demonstration by over 16,000 protestors took place in Sanaʻa on 27 January.[636] On 2 February, President Saleh announced he would not run for reelection in 2013 and that he would not pass power to his son. On 3 February, 20,000 people protested against the government in Sanaʻa,[637] and others in Aden,[638] in a "Day of Rage" called for by Tawakel Karman.[639] On the same day, soldiers, armed members of the General People's Congress and many others held a pro-government counter-demonstration in Sanaʻa.[640]

On February 27, Abdul Malik al-Houthi announced support for the pro-democracy protests and the effort to effect regime change, as had happened in Tunisia and Egypt. Following these statements, large crowds of Houthis joined in protests across Northern Yemen.[641]

Houthi fighters entered Sa'ada on March 19,[642] engaging in a drawn out battle with the pro-government forces of Sheikh Uthman Mujalli.[643] They seized control of the city on March 24[644]after destroying Sheikh Mujalli's house[645]and forcing the local

---

636 "Yemenis in anti-president protest". *Irish Times*. January 27, 2011. Archived from the original on December 4, 2012. Retrieved March 21, 2011.

637 *Daragahi, Borzou (2011-02-03). "Yemen, Middle East: Tens of thousands stage rival rallies in Yemen". latimes.com. Archived from the original on 2012-09-03. Retrieved 2011-02-04.*

Lina Sinjab (2011-01-29). "Yemen protests: 20,000 call for President Saleh to go". BBC News. Archived from the original on 2011-02-03. Retrieved 2011-02-04.

638 "Opposing protesters rally in Yemen". Al Jazeera English. Archived from the original on 2011-02-04. Retrieved 2011-02-04.

639 *"New protests erupt in Yemen". Al Jazeera. 2011-01-29. Archived from the original on 2011-01-31. Retrieved 2011-01-30.*

640 PressTV - Houthis join protests in north Yemen Archived February 25, 2011, at the Wayback Machine

641 PressTV - Houthis join protests in north Yemen Archived February 25, 2011, at the Wayback Machine

642 Sa'ada: A Cry for Help- Yemen Post English Newspaper Online". Archived from the original on 24 August 2014. Retrieved 22 March 2015.

643 "Houthis Control Sa'ada, Help Appoint Governor". Nationalyemen.com. 2011-03-29. Archived from the original on 2015-01-28. Retrieved 2015-01-24.

644 "Insurgents take control of Yemeni city". *Financial Times*. Archivedfrom the original on 5 August 2011. Retrieved 17 October 2014.

645 "Houthis Control Sa'ada, Help Appoint Governor". Nationalyemen.com. 2011-03-29. Archived from the original on 2015-01-28. Retrieved 2015-01-24.

governor to flee.[646] The Houthis established military checkpoints at the entrances to the city[647]after police deserted their posts and were relocated to army camps elsewhere.[648]

On March 26, Houthi rebels declared the creation of their own administration in Saada Governorate, independent from Yemeni authorities. A former arms dealer was appointed governor by the Houthis, the previous governor having fled to Sanaa.[649]

On July 8, 23 people were killed in fighting between the Houthis and the opposition Islah party in al-Jawf governorate. The fighting erupted after the governor of al-Jawf fled, opposition tribes took control of the governorate, and the Houthis refused to hand over a Yemeni military base which they had seized several months earlier. [137] Fighting continued until July 11, with more than 30 people killed.[138] The Houthis claimed that some elements of the pro-Islah militias had links to al-Qaeda.[139]

On July 28, over 120 people were killed as the Houthis launched an offensive to take over government buildings in al-Jawf.[650] Fighting in Jawf lasted for four months, in which time Sunni tribes claimed to have killed 470 Houthis, while acknowledging 85 casualties of their own.[651] The Houthis eventually took control of al-Jawf governorate.[652]

In August a car-bombing killed 14 Houthis in al-Jawf. [143] Although the Houthis initially blamed the US and Israel for the bombing, al-Qaeda eventually claimed

---

646 Yemen Post Staff (27 March 2011). "Houthi Group Appoints Arms Dealer as Governor of Sa'ada province". Yemen Post. Archived from the original on 7 October 2011. Retrieved 27 March 2011

647 Houthis Control Sa'ada, Help Appoint Governor". Nationalyemen.com. 2011-03-29. Archived from the original on 2015-01-28. Retrieved 2015-01-24.

648 Al-Batati, Saeed (2011-03-28). "Yemeni regime loses grip on four provinces". Archived from the original on March 31, 2011. Retrieved March 28, 2011.

649 Yemen Post Staff (27 March 2011). "Houthi Group Appoints Arms Dealer as Governor of Sa'ada province". Yemen Post. Archived from the original on 7 October 2011. Retrieved 27 March 2011.

Al-Batati, Saeed (2011-03-28). "Yemeni regime loses grip on four provinces". Archived from the original on March 31, 2011. Retrieved March 28, 2011.

650 "Yemeni Revolution Slowly entering Phase of War- Yemen Post English Newspaper Online". Archived from the original on 21 October 2014. Retrieved 22 March 2015.

651 "Houthis vs. Islah in al Jawf". Armiesofliberation.com. Archived from the original on 4 October 2011. Retrieved 17 October 2014.

652 "Houthis Close to Control Hajjah Governorate, Amid Expectations of Expansion of Control over Large Parts of Northern Yemen". Islam Times. 2011-11-09. Archived from the original on 2012-04-05. Retrieved 2015-01-24.

responsibility,[653] the organization having declared a holy war against the Houthis earlier that year.[654] In early November clashes erupted between Houthis and a Salafi group in Sa'dah, leaving one Salafist dead.[655]

On November 9, after several days of heavy fighting, the Houthis managed to break through defense lines of the pro-government Kashir and Aahm tribes in Hajjah Governorate, seizing control of the Kuhlan Ash Sharaf District and advancing towards the port of Midi, thereby gaining access to the sea. Through Hajjah, the Houthis would be able to launch an assault on the Yemeni capital Sana'a.[656] By taking Kuhlan Ash Sharaf, the Houthis managed to gain control over a highway linking San'a to the sea[657]

On November 15, clashes between Houthis and Islah party militia restarted in al-Jawf, after an Islah party member tried to blow himself up during the al-Ghadeer festival, in Al Maton District but was captured and killed by the Houthis. A total of 10 people died in the ensuing fighting.[658]

On December 19, Houthis stormed a Sunni Islamist school in the Shaharah District of 'Amran governorate, injuring one teacher and expelling all teachers and students from the school. Houthis then took up positions inside the school.[659]

On 23 November, Saleh signed a power-transfer agreement brokered by the Gulf Cooperation Council in Riyadh, under which he would transfer his power to his Vice-President within 30 days and leave his post as president by February 2012, in exchange for immunity from prosecution.[660] Although the GCC deal was accepted by the JMP, it was rejected by many of the protesters and the Houthis.[661]

653 Al-Qaeda claims attacks on Houthis in northern Yemen Archived August 1, 2011, at the Wayback Machine

654 "Al-Qaeda Announces Holy War against Houthis- Yemen Post English Newspaper Online". Archived from the original on 6 October 2014. Retrieved 22 March 2015.

655 "Clashes in Sa'ada Between Houthis and Salafis- Yemen Post English Newspaper Online". Archived from the original on 19 October 2014. Retrieved 22 March 2015.

656 "Al-Houthi Expansion Plan in Yemen Revealed- Yemen Post English Newspaper Online". Archived from the original on 9 November 2011. Retrieved 22 March 2015.

657 "Houthis Close to Control Hajjah Governorate, Amid Expectations of Expansion of Control over Large Parts of Northern Yemen". Islam Times. 2011-11-09. Archived from the original on 2012-04-05. Retrieved 2015-01-24.

658 "10 Killed in Clashes in N Yemen". English.cri.cn. 15 November 2011. Archived from the original on 28 January 2015. Retrieved 24 January 2015.

659 Houthi militants storm school in Amran". Alsahwa-yemen.net. 2011-12-19. Archived from the original on 2016-03-05. Retrieved 2015-01-24.

660 "Yemen's Saleh signs deal to quit power". The Daily Star Newspaper. Archived from the

"Yemen leader signs power-transfer deal". Al Jazeera English. Archivedfrom the original on 20

A presidential election was held in Yemen on 21 February 2012. With a reported 65 percent turnout, Abdrabbuh Mansur al-Hadi won 99.8% of the vote, and took the oath of office in Yemen's parliament on 25 February 2012. Saleh returned home the same day to attend Hadi's presidential inauguration.[662] After months of protests, Saleh had resigned from the presidency and formally transferred power to his successor, marking the end of his 33-year rule.[663]

Throughout the year, some 200 people were killed in clashes between Houthis and Salafi militias in Sa'dah province.[664]

Post–Saleh (2012–2015)

On February 26, 2012, heavy fighting occurred in Hajjah governorate as Houthis fought Sunni tribesmen loyal to the Al-Islah party. At least seven fighters from the Hojjor tribe were killed and nine others injured, while in the Ahem area nine bodies were found, belonging to Houthi fighters. Houthis launched an assault backed by artillery on al-Jarabi area, al-Hazan village, al-Moshaba mountain, and Ahem police station to take control of the al-Moshaba mountain. Parts of the Kushar District were put under siege[157] since clashes erupted in that province between Houthis and the al-Zakari tribe in November.[158] In early February, over 55 people had been killed during sectarian violence in Kushar[665]During February and March some 27 people were killed and 36 injured due to mines in Hajjah. A total of 600 were killed in clashes in Hajjah between November 2011 and April 2012, mainly in Kushar and Mustaba Districts.[666]

On March 8, Houthi gunmen in the northern province of Amran killed a high-ranking military commander and six of his bodyguards.[667]

661 *"Process of withdrawing troops and armed tribesmen started for enhancing peace and normalizing life in Yemen"*. Yobserver.com. Archived from *the original* on 2013-01-05. Retrieved 2012-11-07.

"Houthis' Leader: US, Allies Plot to Spark Sectarian Rift in Yemen". Fars News Agency. 2011-12-20. Archived from *the original* on 2012-06-01. Retrieved 2012-11-07

662 Kasinof, Laura (27 February 2012). "Yemen Swears In New President to the Sound of Applause, and Violence". *The New York Times*. Archived from the original on 10 November 2012. Retrieved 15 August 2012.

663 "Yemen's Saleh formally steps down after 33 years". AFP. 2012-02-27. Archived from the original on 2012-05-25. Retrieved 2012-11-07.

664 Situations calm down in north of Yemen after 16 fighters killedArchived 2013-02-10 at Archive.today

665 Sectarian clashes continue in north Yemen, at least 55 killed". www.uruknet.info. Archived from the original on 2015-01-08. Retrieved 2015-01-24.

666 United Nations High Commissioner for Refugees (2012-04-18). "Yemen: Rising landmine death toll in Hajjah Governorate". UNHCR. Retrieved 2015-01-24.

667 *"Yemen: military commander, six bodyguards killed by Houthis- Yemen Post English Newspaper Online"*. Archived from the original on 2 April 2015. Retrieved 22 March 2015.

On March 23, a suicide bomber targeted a Houthi march in Sa'dah, no casualties were reported.[668] On March 25, some 14 people were killed and three injured in a car bombing in al-Hazm of al-Jawf province, targeting a Shi'a gathering near a school.[669] Salafis killed another 8 Houthis in an attack on April 21.[670] From June 2 to June 4, Houthis clashed with Salafi militias in Kataf district leaving several dead.[671] Houthis claim to have taken over three Salafi positions and confiscated Saudi weapons during the clash.[672]

On August 21, clashes broke out between Houthis and tribes in Ash Shahil District of Hajjah after Houthis allegedly shot two women in the district. As the fighting broke out, Houthis retreated from al-Amroor area and retreated to the mountains between Janeb al-Sham and Janeb al-Yemen. Houthis were said to control several mountains in the region including mount Azzan and the governorate center that overlooks al-Mahabishah, Qafl Shamer and Ku'aydinah Districts. A truce was signed between the two sides on August 30.[673] Clashes reignited on September 6 and Houthis managed to seize control of five schools, a medical center and a police station. Some 30 people were killed in the battles.[674] Afterwards Houthis claimed civilian areas were being shelled by al-Islah, while MP Ali al-Ma'amari accused Houthis of killing a worker from Taiz.[675]

In September and October, Houthis led many protests in Sana'a as part of the 2012 Anti-US protests caused by the release of Innocence of Muslims. Houthi slogans were hung all across the old city of Sana'a and Shi'a majority areas during the protests.[676] This led to Houthis expanding their control in Sana'a Governorate and other areas

668 "Suicide bomber kills 12 in northern Yemen". *Chicago Tribune*. 2012-05-25. Archived from the original on 2012-11-01. Retrieved 2012-11-19.

669 "Suicide bombing kills 14 Houthis in Al-Jawf". Archived from the original on 3 June 2013. Retrieved 22 March 2015.

670 "PressTV - Salafi attack on Houthis kills eight in Yemen". Archived from the original on 2012-07-09. Retrieved 2012-11-19.

671 "Clashes renewed between Houthis and Salfis - Yemen Post English Newspaper Online". Archived from the original on 24 August 2014. Retrieved 22 March 2015.

672 "Houthis take control of three positions in north Yemen, claim confiscating Saudi weapons". 20 June 2012. Archived from the original on 20 June 2012.

673 *"Truce shook on between Houthis, Al-Shahel tribesmen in Hajja"*. *Yemen Times*. Archived from the original on 24 March 2015. Retrieved 22 March2015.

674 Houthis Fight Tribes, Take over Schools, Public Offices in Yemen, Site - Yemen Post English Newspaper Online". Archived from the original on 6 October 2014. Retrieved 22 March 2015

675 "HugeDomains.com - FnaYemen.com is for sale (Fna Yemen)". *www.hugedomains.com*. Archived from the original on 2018-11-19. Retrieved 2019-04-13.

676 Hammond, Andrew (2012-10-03). "FEATURE-Houthi rebels seen gaining new influence in Yemen". Reuters. Archived from the original on 2015-10-10. Retrieved 2017-07-01.

around the capital, particularly Khwlan and Sanhan Districts and the town Shibam Kawkaban in al-Mahwit.[677] Al-Juraf district was also named as a Houthi stronghold, where they had large numbers of weapons stationed. Sunni sources have alleged that Houthis have used the protests to smuggle weapons and fighters from areas surrounding Sana'a into Sana'a city itself, mainly in the old city.[678]

During one of the protests, in Raydah, Amran, clashes broke out between Houthis and Islahi gunmen after the Islahi gunmen interrupted a Houthi mass rally, denouncing Innocence of Muslims and the US government, on September 21. Two people were killed during the clash and three Islahi gunmen were captured.[679] Fighting continued until September 23, leaving 16 fighters dead and 36 Islah men captured by the Houthis. After a cease-fire was agreed on, Houthis withdrew from the town and released the prisoners they had taken.[680] A group of Houthis remained in Owaidan mosque.[681]

2014–15: Victory for the insurgency

Battle of Sana'a (2014) and Houthi takeover in Yemen

On 18 August 2014, the Houthis began a series of demonstrations in Sana'a against increased fuel prices. On 21 September, the Houthis took control of Sana'a, after which Prime Minister Mohammed Basindawa resigned and the Houthis signed a deal for a new unity government with other political parties. The protests were marked by clashes between the Houthis and the government and also clashes between the Houthis and al-Qaeda in the Arabian Peninsula.[682] At least 340 people were killed on the outskirts of the Yemeni capital in one week of fighting between the Shiite rebels and Sunni militiamen before the city fell[683]The new government was sworn in on 9

677 Yemen Fox. "Yemen Fox- Houthis seek to take control over Sana'a". Archived from the original on 2 April 2015. Retrieved 22 March 2015
"HugeDomains.com - FnaYemen.com is for sale (Fna Yemen)". *www.hugedomains.com*. Archived from the original on 2018-11-19. Retrieved 2019-04-1

678 "HugeDomains.com - FnaYemen.com is for sale (Fna Yemen)". *www.hugedomains.com*. Archived from the original on 2018-11-19. Retrieved 2019-04-13.

679 Yemen Fox. "Yemen Fox- Mohammed Jumaih - Houthis in Sana'a". Archived from the original on 2 April 2015. Retrieved 22 March 2015.

680 Situations calm down in north of Yemen after 16 fighters killedArchived 2013-02-10 at Archive.today

681 *Yemen Fox. "Yemen Fox- Mediation ends war, drives Houthis out of Raida". Archived from the original on 2 April 2015. Retrieved 22 March2015.*

682 *Frank Gardner (24 October 2014). "Frank Gardner: Yemen at risk of civil war, says ambassador". BBC. Archived from the original on 30 October 2014. Retrieved 29 October 2014.*

683 "At least 340 killed in Yemen's week-long fighting". *The Daily Star Newspaper*. Archived from the original on 2015-10-13. Retrieved 2014-09-22.

November, although the Houthis and General People's Congress announced they would not take part.[684]

A spokesman for the Houthi group has accused Yemen's President Hadi of arming members of Al-Qaeda in the Marib province, east of the country, in order to create a new security crisis.[685]

The crisis intensified as Houthi militants attacked the presidential palace and private residence in January 2015, quickly seizing control of both. On 22 January, President Abdrabbuh Mansur Hadi and his ministers resigned.[686] The Houthis declared themselves in full control of the government on 6 February, dissolving parliament and putting a Revolutionary Committee led by Mohammed Ali al-Houthi in charge of the country.[687]

Aftermath
Aftermath of the Houthi takeover in Yemen

Hadi escaped from house arrest on 21 February and made his way to Aden, where he renounced his resignation, condemned the Houthi takeover, and attempted to reassemble his government. He declared Aden to be Yemen's provisional capital.

Fighting broke out over Aden International Airport on 19 March after Hadi dismissed a general in Aden, Abdul-Hafez al-Saqqaf, whom he suspected of being loyal to Ali Abdullah Saleh, widely believed to be an ally of the Houthis.[688] The next day, a quadruple suicide bombing ripped through two mosques in Sanaʻa while hundreds of Houthis were praying there. The Revolutionary Committee declared a "state of general mobilisation" in response to the events and launched a military offensive directed at Hadi's holdouts, whom the Houthis accused of being in league with al-Qaeda.[689]

Since the clashes at the airport and the Houthis' southward offensive, the media has increasingly described the deteriorating situation in Yemen and the escalating clashes

---

684 "Yemen swears in new government amid boycott". Al Jazeera. 9 November 2014. Archived from the original on 11 November 2014. Retrieved 14 November 2014.

685 Houthis accuse Yemen's president of arming Al-Qaeda". *Middle East Monitor - The Latest from the Middle East*. Archived from the original on 8 February 2015. Retrieved 22 March 2015.

686 "Yemen President Hadi Resigns After Shiite Rebels Seize Palace". Bloomberg. 22 January 2015. Archived from the original on 23 January 2015. Retrieved 22 January 2015.

687 Yemen's Shia rebels finalize coup, vow to dissolve parliament". *The Globe and Mail*. 6 February 2015. Archived from the original on 19 July 2015. Retrieved 6 February 2015

688 *Onyanga-Omara, Jane (19 March 2015). "Clashes force closure of Yemen's Aden airport". USA TODAY. Archived from the original on 24 March 2015. Retrieved 31 March 2015.*

689 *Saba News Agency. 21 March 2015. Archived from the original on 23 March 2015.*

"Q&A: Yemen's slide into civil war". Financial Times. 22 March 2015. Retrieved 8 April 2015

between the two factions claiming to represent the legitimate government as a civil war.[690]

Several states led by Saudi Arabia also mounted a military intervention in Yemen codenamed "Operation Decisive Storm". The Saudi-led coalition sided with Hadi's government in Aden, shelling Houthi positions from land and sea and hitting them with airstrikes.[691]

Missile attacks on Saudi territory

On May 19, 2017 Saudi Arabia intercepted a Houthi-fired ballistic missile targeting, a deserted area south of the Saudi capital and most populous city Riyadh.[692] This missile attack was followed by another one on 27 October 2017, allegedly aimed towards the Holy Mosque in Mecca (*"Makkah Al-Mukarramah, the prayer direction of Muslims and the Cradle of Revelation"*), which was condemned by a special Emergency Meeting of the Council of Foreign Ministers of the Member States of the Organization of Islamic Cooperation (OIC) on 17 November 2017.

On 19 December 2017, a direct attack on Riyadh by another ballistic missile was intercepted, allegedly*"Iranian-made"*, launched by*"Iranian-supported rebels"* and aimed at the Saudi royal palace.[693] Another special Extraordinary Meeting of the Council of Foreign Ministers of the Member States of the OIC on 21 January 2018

---

690 *Q&A: Yemen's slide into civil war". Financial Times. 22 March 2015. Retrieved 8 April 2015.*

Yemen crisis: Shortage of water and medical supplies threatens civilians caught up in devastating civil war". The Independent. 8 April 2015. Archived from the original on 11 April 2015. Retrieved 8 April 2015.

Holtz, Michael (7 April 2015). "Warnings of humanitarian crisis as Yemen's civil war rolls on (+video)". The Christian Science Monitor. Archived from the original on 8 April 2015. Retrieved 8 April 2015.

Aboudi, Sami. "Yemenis forced to take to sea from Aden as civil war rages through ancient port". Japan Times. Archived from the original on 2016-01-19. Retrieved 2015-04-09.

691 Saudi and Arab allies bomb Houthi positions in Yemen". Al Jazeera. 25 March 2015. Archived from the original on 26 March 2015. Retrieved 26 March 2015.

692 *(www.dw.com), Deutsche Welle. "Saudi Arabia intercepts Houthi rebel missile fired towards Riyadh - News - DW - 20.05.2017". DW.COM. Archived from the original on 2018-01-19. Retrieved 2018-01-29.*

2. ^ *News, ABC. "ABC News". ABC News. Archived from the original on 2017-05-24. Retrieved 2018-01-29.*

693 *Hubbard, Ben; Cumming-Bruce, Nick (19 December 2017). "Rebels in Yemen Fire Second Ballistic Missile at Saudi Capital". The New York Times. Archived from the original on 23 January 2018. Retrieved 29 January 2018.*

Wintour, Patrick; Dehghan, Saeed Kamali (19 December 2017). "Saudi Arabia shoots down Houthi missile aimed at Riyadh palace". The Guardian. Archived from the original on 29 January 2018. Retrieved 29 January 2018 – via www.theguardian.com.

in Jeddah condemned the attack, decrying it as an aggression on the KSA, and taking it as *"evidence of the Iranian-backed Houthi militias' refusal to cooperate with the international community and accept international resolutions"*, referring to the resolution adopted in the Mecca Conference in November 2016 and relevant UN Security Council resolutions.

On 26 March 2018, Houthis fired 7 ballistic missiles towards the Saudi capital of Riyadh, all of which were intercepted by Saudi systems. An Egyptian man was killed and 2 injured as a result.[694]

On 23 June 2019, Houthi rebels carried out a drone attack on Abha International Airport, killing a Syrian national and wounding 21.

In June 2019 the Saudi-led coalition stated that the Houthis had launched 226 ballistic missiles during the insurgency so far.[695]

On September 14, 2019, the Houthi rebels claimed the Abqaiq and Khurais drone attacks, which caused massive damage to Saudi oil facilities.[696]

Iran, North Korea and Hezbollah

There have been a number of allegations that Iran, North Korea and Hezbollah have intervened to aid the Houthis, including:

The Saudi and Yemeni governments both accuse Iran of helping the Houthis. Iran, they say, has secretly landed arms on the Red Sea coast. In October, 2009, Yemen's government said its navy intercepted an arms-carrying Iranian vessel. Yemen's state-controlled press claims Houthi rebels have been trained in an Iranian-run camp across the Red Sea in Eritrea. Yemen's president, Ali Abdullah Saleh, says members of Lebanon's Iran-backed Hezbollah militia are teaching them. The Yemeni authorities also darkly note that the Houthis' long-time leader, Hussein Badreddin al-Houthi, who died in battle in 2004, used to visit Qom, one of Shia Islam's holiest places.[697] None of these accusations have yet been borne out by independent observers and the Iranians deny any involvement.

"Yemen rebels fire missile at Riyadh". BBC News. 19 December 2017. *Archived* from the original on 6 July 2018. Retrieved 21 July 2018 – via www.bbc.com

694 Amir Vera; Nic Robertson. *"Saudi Arabia intercepts 7 missiles fired from Yemen, military officials say"*. CNN. Retrieved 2018-03-26.

"The Associated Press on Twitter". Twitter. Retrieved 2018-03-26

695 Lisa Barrington; Aziz El Yaakoubi (17 September 2019). *"Yemen Houthi drones, missiles defy years of Saudi air strikes"*. Reuters. Retrieved 27 September 2019.

696 Business, John Defterios and Victoria Cavaliere, CNN. *"Drone strikes knock out half of Saudi oil capacity, 5 million barrels a day"*. CNN. Retrieved 2019-09-14.

697 *"Yemen's war: Pity those caught in the middle"*. The Economist. *Archived* from the original on 11 February 2010. Retrieved 17 October 2014.

Saudi-owned Al Arabiya claimed that "well-informed sources" are saying that "the president of the former South Yemen (Ali Salim al-Bidh) conducted a secret visit to the Lebanese capital Beirut last October (2009), and tried to contact figures close to Hezbollah aiming to win its support for the Houthi rebels, and for South (Yemen's) secession." The sources added that those Hezbollah-allied figures "informed al-Bidh that the party's top officials do not want to meet with him and that they do not approve the attribution of Hezbollah's name with what is happening in Yemen, or to appear as supporting to any rebellion." Ibrahim al-Mussawi, Head of Hezbollah's Media Unit, told Alarabiya.net that his party denies the report about an alleged secret visit.[698]

High-ranking officials from the Iranian Revolutionary Guard were said to havsecretly met with Houthi rebels and Hezbollah in Yemen to coordinate joint military operations against Saudi positions along the border. Pan-Arab Asharq al-Awsat daily said Arab and Egyptian sources uncovered that a number of intelligence services in the region have learned of the three-way meeting which also aimed at developing a plan to escalate the military situation along the Saudi-Yemeni border. It said the high-level meeting which took place in November, 2009 was the most prominent evidence of "direct Iranian involvement" in the support of Houthi rebels financially, militarily and logistically.[699]

Yemeni Foreign Minister Abu Bakr al-Qirbi on 13 December 2009 urged Iran to crack down on Iranian groups he accused of aiding Houthi rebels in northern Yemen and held Iran's government partly to blame. He said: "Religious (Shiite) circles and groups in Iran are providing aid to the Huthis," However, Iran has repeatedly denied such accusations.[700]

On 25 May 2009, Iran first deployed warships to the Gulf of Aden to combat piracy in Somalia.[701] On 18 November, a second group of Iranian warships came to the Gulf of Aden, at the same time as Saudi Arabia imposed a blockade on Houthi-controlled coasts and launched a crackdown on Houthi ships delivering weapons to the Houthis.[702] Iran dispatched its 5th fleet to the Gulf of Aden.[703] Some have alleged that the Iranian Navy is operating there to help supply the Houthis with weapons and counter the Saudi naval power in the area rather than to fight Somali pirates.[201]

---

698 Hizbullah Denies Report about Former South Yemen President Visiting Beirut to Demand Support for Huthis". *Naharnet*. Retrieved 17 October 2014.

699 Secret Meeting in Yemen between Iran, Huthi, Hizbullah Officials". *Naharnet*. Retrieved 17 October 2014

700 Yemeni FM: Iran Must Curb Groups Aiding Huthi Rebels *"Yemeni FM: Iran Must Curb Groups Aiding Huthi Rebels". naharnet. 2009-12-13.*

701 Iran Sends 6 Warships to International Waters in 'Saber Rattling' Move". Fox News. 2009-05-25. Archived from the original on 2012-10-22. Retrieved 2010-02-06.

702 Iran Sends 6 Warships to International Waters in 'Saber Rattling' Move". Fox News. 2009-05-25. Archived from the original on 2012-10-22. Retrieved 2010-02-06.

703 Archived copy". Archived from the original on 2010-01-25. Retrieved 2010-02-06.

According to a recent UN report made in August 2018, the North Korean government-owned Korean Ministry of Military Equipment and Korea Mining and Development Trading Corporation (KOMID) are supplying the Houthis with arms which violated North Korea's sanctions[704]

Saudi Arabia, Egypt, Jordan, Sudan, Bahrain, and the United Arab Emirates.

Saudi Arabia has led a major military intervention in Yemen, and organized a coalition of other nations to support its efforts, including Egypt, Jordan, Sudan, and Bahrain.[705]

United States

In December 2009, *The New York Times* reported that the United States has provided weapons and logistical support to Yemeni government strikes against suspected hide-outs of Al Qaeda within its borders. The officials said that the American support was approved by President Obama and came at the request of the Yemeni government.[706]

Houthi leaders however claim that US involvement started on 14 December when the US launched 28 air raids.[707] At least 120 people were killed and 44 injured by the alleged US air raids on the regions of Amran, Hajjah and Sa'ada in North Yemen, a Houthi leader was quoted as saying: "The US air force perpetrated an appalling massacre against citizens in the north of Yemen as it launched air raids on various populated areas, markets, refugee camps and villages along with Saudi warplanes. The savage crime committed by the US air force shows the real face of the United States. It cancels out much touted American claims of human rights protection, promotion of freedoms of citizens as well as democracy."[708] The Houthi claimed that new air raids on 18 December killed 63 civilians, including 28 children and injured at least 90 people.[709]

On June 17, 2011, following Friday prayers, tens of thousands of protestors rallied in Sa'dah against US interference in Yemen.[207]

---

704 North Korea has not stopped nuclear, missile program: confidential U.N. report". Reuters. 2018-08-03. Archived from the original on 2018-12-06. Retrieved 2018-12-06.

705 The Saudi Arabia-Yemen War of 2015". *The Atlantic*. 2015-05-07. Archived from the original on 2017-02-28. Retrieved 2017-03-07.

706 Shanker, Thom; Landler, Mark (18 December 2009). "U.S. Aids Yemeni Raids on Al Qaeda, Officials Say". *New York Times*. Archived from the original on 26 July 2016. Retrieved 24 February 2017.

707 US fighter jets attack Yemeni fighters". Press TV. 14 December 2009. Archived from the original on 2 January 2010. Retrieved 29 December 2009

708 US fighters pound Sa'ada, kill 120". Press TV. 16 December 2009. Archived from the original on 19 December 2009. Retrieved 29 December2009.

709 US air raids kill 63 civilians in Yemen". Press TV. 18 December 2009. Archived from the original on 2016-01-19. Retrieved 29 December 2009.

The Houthis blamed US intelligence forces of carrying out a bombing in August 2011 which killed 14 Houthi fighters.[208]

Other issues

Jordan: It has been alleged that Jordan deployed commandos to fight alongside the Saudis during their offensive in Northern Mount Al-Dukhan and that Saudis sent the Jordanian commandos to fight in Northern Yemen. They also sent auxiliary units to support Saudi forces.[710] By December 2009 it was alleged that over 2,000 Jordanian soldiers were fighting at the front[711]

Morocco: It was alleged that Morocco have sent hundreds of elite fighters, mainly para-troopers trained for counter-insurgency operations, to aid the 2009–2010 Saudi offensive.[712]

Pakistan: Initially it was alleged in some news channels that the Pakistan government had sent contingent of special forces to join Yemeni counter insurgency operations in Sa'dah. However, Pakistan government has strongly rejected these rumors of sending Pakistani troops to join a Saudi-backed coalition forces fighting Houthi rebels in war-stricken Yemen. The official statement says Government of Pakistan is in favor of a peaceful solution to this dispute.[713]

Human rights violations during the Yemeni Civil War (2015-present)

In April 2008, the United Nations High Commissioner for Refugees estimated that the conflict had created 77,000 internally displaced persons (IDPs) in Sa'dah Governorate.[714] By order of then king Abdullah of Saudi Arabia, the Saudis were to shelter and build 10,000 new homes for the war-displaced people of Saudi nationality in Jizan.[715]

---

710 Jordanian commandos join war on Houthi fighters". *Press TV*. 21 November 2009. Archived from the original on 23 November 2009. Retrieved 29 December 2009.

711 Canales, Pedro (3 December 2009). "Marruecos y Jordania envían tropas de élite para ayudar a los saudíes en Yemen". *El Imparcial* (in Spanish). Archived from the original on 7 December 2009. Retrieved 29 December 2009.

712 Canales, Pedro (3 December 2009). "Marruecos y Jordania envían tropas de élite para ayudar a los saudíes en Yemen". *El Imparcial* (in Spanish). Archived from the original on 7 December 2009. Retrieved 29 December 2009.

713 Suspected al-Qaida car bomb kills 14 Shi'ite Houthi rebels in Yemen: official". Archived from the original on 15 November 2013. Retrieved 22 March 2015.

714 YEMEN: Rebel leader calls for international aid". IRIN. 2008-05-06. Archived from the original on 2009-06-17. Retrieved 2008-05-23.

715 *Saudi king visits area of Yemen border conflict". Al Arabiya. 2 December 2009. Archived from the original on 19 December 2009. Retrieved 29 December 2009.*

Use of child soldiers

Unicef and the Islamic relief were reported as condemning Houthi rebels for abusing children by forcing them to fight for their cause.[716] In November 2009, over 400 children walked to the UNDP office in Sana'a, to protest against the alleged Houthi abuse of children's rights.[717]

Allegations were made that both the Yemeni government and the Houthi rebels exploited the use of child soldiers during the war. Human Rights Watch noted difficulty in citing the exact numbers of child soldiers on the Houthis' part. However, there existed a significant amount of evidence that the government itself employed child soldiers in the ranks of the armed forces, the result of the country's lack of birth certificates and further documentation of age.[718] Where the Yemeni government was

"10,000 houses for Jazan displaced". *Arab News*. 3 December 2009. *Archived* from the original on 30 December 2009. Retrieved 29 December2009.

"Saudi king orders construction of 10,000 houses for displaced people in south". *Kuwait News Agency*. 2 December 2009. Archived from *the original* on 19 September 2011. Retrieved 29 December 2009.

716 *"UN calls for the prosecution of child soldier recruiters"*. The National. Archived from *the original* on 14 January 2013. Retrieved 17 October 2014.

"Issue of child soldiers raised in Yemen". UPI. *Archived* from the original on 17 October 2014. Retrieved 17 October 2014.

"Yemen child soldier tells of his hatred for al-Houthi rebels". The Times. *Archived* from the original on 14 August 2011. Retrieved 17 October 2014.

717 Yemen children renews protest al-Houthi-related child abuse". 5 April 2011. Archived from *the original* on 5 April 2011.

718 *All Quiet On The Northern Front?"* (PDF). March 2010. Retrieved 2010-09-24.[permanent dead link]

"UN calls for the prosecution of child soldier recruiters". The National. 2010-02-13. Archived from *the original* on 2016-01-19. Retrieved 2010-09-21.

limited by restrictions, The Times reported on a fourteen-year-old boy who fought for a tribal militia sponsored by the government.[719]

A Sanaʿa-based human rights group, Seyaj Organization for Childhood Protection, noted that the Houthis were mainly responsible, stating that fifty-percent of the rebels were under the age of eighteen. It is estimated that anywhere between 400 and 500 children are killed every year in Yemen as the result of tribal conflict.[720] The same organization eventually released a report claiming that 700 children were used as soldiers by the Houthis and pro-government militias during the war. The report concluded that 187 children were killed during the conflict, 71% as the result of the fighting.[222]

These allegations were supported by the story of "Akram," a nine-year-old boy who was duped by a cousin to deliver a bomb to an unspecified target in the Old City of Saada. Akram, unknowingly wired with an explosive, was apprehended by police and taken to safety in Sanaʿa, along with his father. A day after telling his story at a press conference Akram's home was bombed in Saada City. His younger brother suffered injuries in the retaliation.[721]

Saudi Arabia has also been accused of using child soldiers from Darfur in the frontline of Yemen war.[722]

- **Conclusion**

Saudi Arabia has long accused Iran of arming the Houthis to fight a proxy war. "We are worried about…the tendencies of Iran in the region, which is one of the leading elements implanting instability in the region," the late Saudi Foreign Minister, Prince Saud al Faisal, said in 2015. In April 2017, Secretary of State Rex Tillerson said that Iran supports the Houthis' "attempted overthrow of the government by providing military equipment, funding, and training, thus threatening Saudi Arabia's southern border." In November 2017, however, Revolutionary Guards commander Maj. Gen. Ali Jafari claimed that "Iran's assistance is at the level of advisory and spiritual support." Tensions over Iranian support of the Houthis escalated in late 2017. In November, Saudi Arabia charged Iran with an act of war for a missile fired at the Saudi capital by the Houthis in Yemen. Iran denied any links to the attack. But remnants of four ballistic missiles fired into Saudi Arabia by the Houthis on May 19, July 22, July 26 and November 4, 2017 appear to have been designed and manufactured by Iran, according to a confidential U.N. report from November 2017.

---

719 Evans, Judith (2009-10-10). "Yemen child soldier tells of his hatred for al-Houthi rebels". *The Times*. London. Archived from the original on 2011-08-14. Retrieved 2010-09-24.

720 Yemen's child soldiers go to war". UPI. 2010-01-06. Archived from the original on 2010-04-03. Retrieved 2010-09-19.

721 The children of Yemen's tribal war". The Sunday Herald. 2009-12-05. Archived from the original on 2010-11-25. Retrieved 2010-09-19.

722 Child soldiers from Darfur fighting at front line of war in Yemen, returned soldiers say". *The Independent*. 2018-12-29. Archived from the original on 2018-12-30. Retrieved 2019-01-19.

"The United States welcomes this report, as should every nation concerned about Iranian expansion," U.S. ambassador to the United Nations Nikki Haley said on December 14, in front of the remains of a missile allegedly fired by the Houthis into Saudi Arabia. "It was made in Iran, then sent to Houthi militants in Yemen. From there it was fired at a civilian airport, with the potential to kill hundreds of innocent civilians in Saudi Arabia."Iranian officials and Houthi leaders denied U.S. claims. "After three years of war, America all of a sudden reaches to the conclusion to finf evidence that Iran supports the Houthis," Yemeni authorities have however supported the idea that "America did not find any evidence in all the missiles fired from Yemen until now. The story is clear. They want to give Arabs a story to divert their attention from Jerusalem. Instead being angry at Israel, they wave the Iranian boy," On December 21, the U.S. State Department echoed Haley's allegations. "There is a very key relationship between the Iranians and the Houthis," They don't want to overstate it. I don't want to suggest that the Houthis operate entirely at the behest of the Iranians. But it's an important relationship and one that the Iranians are able to exploit." While U.N. report concluded Iran had violated an arms embargo by failing to prevent the Houthis from obtaining Iranian missiles. Iran did not comment on the U.N. panel report, but Iranian foreign minister Javad Zarif denied U.S. claims of Tehran's missile support once again in a series of tweets in late January 2018. Meanwhile In mid-February, the United States, Britain, and France drafted a UN resolution that condemned Iran for violating the Yemen arms embargo by failing to prevent the Houthis from obtaining Iranian missiles. Russia vetoed the resolution. he Houthis stepped up their attacks on Saudi Arabia in the following months. In late March, the rebels fired seven missiles at Saudi Arabia in one night and resulted in the of an Egyptian resident. A few weeks later, they struck a Saudi oil tanker in international waters west of Yemen's Hodeidah port. A mid-April missile targeting the Saudi capital Riyadh prompted a U.S. response. The State Department condemned the attack and blamed Iran for its alleged Houthi support. "Americans believe that they support the right of their Saudi partners to defend their borders against these threats, which are fueled by the Iranian regime's dangerous proliferation of weapons and destabilizing activities in the region," Hussein Abdreddin al Houthi, a prominent Zaydi cleric and member of parliament from 1993 to 1997, became a strong critic of President Ali Abudllah Saleh in the 1990s. He **accused** the government of aligning too closely with the United States and Israel. Tensions mounted further after President Saleh reportedly **cut** funding to Hussein al Houthi in 2000. Frustrated by the Zaydis' poor political and economic status, he began rallying supporters for anti-government demonstrations in the early 2000s. The government issued a warrant for al Houthi's arrest, and his followers began clashing violently with security forces. Al Houthi was **killed** by security forces in 2004. Since then, his relatives and supporters have waged six uprisings against the government, known as the Houthi wars. President Saleh accused **Iran** of supporting the rebellions. The Houthis signed a **ceasefire** agreement with the government in 2010, but joined the Arab Spring protests against Saleh about a year later.

The Houthis have other sources of support, however. They have reportedly received funding from local supporters and sympathetic charities as well as from illegal trade. Hussein Abdreddin al Houthi, a prominent Zaydi cleric and member of parliament from 1993 to 1997, became a strong critic of President Ali Abudllah Saleh in the 1990s. He accused the government of aligning too closely with the United States and Israel. Tensions mounted further after President Saleh reportedly cut funding to Hussein al Houthi in 2000. Frustrated by the Zaydis' poor political and economic status, he began rallying supporters for anti-government demonstrations in the early 2000s. The government issued a warrant for al Houthi's arrest, and his followers began clashing violently with security forces. Al Houthi was killed by security forces in 2004. Since then, his relatives and supporters have waged six uprisings against the government, known as the Houthi wars. President Saleh accused Iran of supporting the rebellions. The Houthis signed a ceasefire agreement with the government in 2010, but joined the Arab Spring protests against Saleh one year later. Foreign Minister Javad Zarif accused the United States of fabricating evidence related to the displayed missile parts recovered from Saudi Arabia.

What is the relationship between Houthis and other Islamists in Yemen?

The Houthis have a tense relationship with Islah, a Sunni Islamist party with links to the Muslim Brotherhood. Islah claims the Houthis are an Iranian **proxy**, and blames them for sparking unrest in Yemen. The Houthis, on the other hand, have **accused** Islah of cooperating with al Qaeda in the Arabian Peninsula (AQAP).

After the Houthis took over Sanaa in September 2014, Islah initially took a few **steps** towards reconciliation. In November, top Islah and Houthi leaders met to discuss a political partnership. Islah called on the Houthis to cease attacks on Islah members and to release Islah prisoners. In December, the United Nations and Gulf Cooperation Council brokered a **deal** between the two groups to cease hostilities.

But clashes between the Houthis and Islah continued. In the first four months of 2015, the Houthis kidnapped dozens of Islah party leaders and raided their offices. By April, more than 100 Islah leaders were detained by the Houthis. Tensions increased after Islah declared **support** for the Saudi-led airstrikes.

The Houthis are also at odds with Sunni extremist groups. On March 20, 2015, an ISIS affiliate calling itself the Sanaa Province claimed responsibility for suicide bomb attacks on two Zaydi mosques that killed at least 135 people and injured more than 300 others. The group issued a **statement** that said "infidel Houthis should know that the soldiers of the Islamic State will not rest until they eradicate them."

AQAP denied involvement in the mosque attacks, but has frequently targeted the Houthis. In April 2015, the group claimed responsibility for three suicide attacks that **killed** dozens of Houthis in Abyan, al Bayda', and Lahij. AQAP has reportedly partnered with southern **tribes** to fight the Houthis.

Who leads Houthis ?

Abdul Malik al Houthi, brother of Hussein al Houthi, has been the group's spiritual, military, and political leader since **2007**. Little is known of his personal life, and he makes few public appearances. His brother-in-law, Youssef al Midani, is the **deputy** leader. Abdul Malik's two brothers, Yahia and Abdul-Karim, are also senior **leaders** of the movement.

On April 14, 2015 the U.S. Treasury imposed sanctions on Abdul Malik al Houthi for engaging in acts that "threaten the peace, security, or stability of Yemen." The same month, the U.N. Security Council imposed an arms embargo against the Houthis and blacklisted Abdul Malik al Houthi.

Timeline: The Houthis in Yemen
2014

Sept. 21-22: Houthi rebels storm Sanaa and seize government buildings. The UN brokers a deal requiring Hadi to form a new government.

Nov. 1: Houthi rebels attack the al Islah party headquarters in the southwestern city of Ibb.

Nov. 7-8: Hadi announces a new cabinet, but the Houthis reject it.

Nov. 28: Houthi rebels and al Islah reach a deal agreeing to cease hostilities, but clashes between the groups continue.

Dec. 14: Houthi rebels blow up a building belonging to al Islah in Sanaa.

Dec. 20: Dozens of protestors gather in Sanaa to demand that Houthi rebels leave the capital. Houthis respond by abducting activist Shadi Khasrouf, who participated in the protests.

2015
Jan. 22: Hadi resigns under pressure from Houthi rebels.

March 20: Suicide attacks targeting two Houthi mosques in Sanaa kill more than 130 people and injure more than 300 others.

March 26: Saudi Arabia begins launching airstrikes in Yemen, coordinating with a 10-nation coalition.

Sept. 22: Hadi returns to Aden after the Houthis are driven out.

Dec. 15: U.N.-sponsored peace talks **begin** in Geneva, Switzerland and a ceasefire goes into effect in Yemen.

2016

Jan. 7: Iran **claims** Saudi warplanes attacked Iran's embassy in Sanaa. The Saudi-led coalition and Yemen's government **deny** that the embassy building was targeted.

April 21: U.N.-backed talks **begin** in Kuwait between the Houthis and President Abd-Rabbu Mansour Hadi's government.

Aug. 7: U.N.-backed talks in Kuwait conclude without an agreement between the Houthis and Hadi's government.

Oct. 19-21: War parties**agree** to a 72-hour ceasefire, allowing for civilian access to humanitarian aid. The ceasefire holds for 3 days, and Saudi-led coalition airstrikes recommence shortly after the truce expires.

Oct. 27: U.N. Yemen envoy Ismail Ould Cheikh Ahmed **proposes** a new peace plan aimed at ending the conflict. It calls for members of the internationally-recognized Hadi government to step down or accept diminished roles in exchange for a Houthi withdrawal from major cities.

Oct. 31: U.S. ambassador to the United Nations, Samantha Power, **calls** for an end to indiscriminate Saudi-led coalition airstrikes in Yemen.

Nov. 29: The Houthis and members of the ousted President Ali Abdullah Saleh's General People's Congress **form** a new 35-minister government based in Sanaa.

2017

Jan. 18: A Houthi strike **kills** six civilians in the central city of Taiz, just one day after the killing of six other civilians outside of the city.

Jan. 23: Yemeni government forces**seizing** control of the Red Sea port of Mokha after launching an assault against and **pushing** out Houthi rebels.

Jan. 30: Three Houthi suicide boats **attack** a Saudi frigate off the Hodeida port in the Red Sea, killing two crew members and wounding three others.

Jan. 31: The Houthis' official news agency **says** they launched a ballistic missile at a Saudi-led coalition military base on the Red Sea island of Zuqar on Monday, countering the Saudi claim of a suicide attack.

Feb. 22: A senior Yemeni army general is **killed** in a missile attack by the Houthis.

March 25: A court in Houthi-controlled territory **sentences** President Hadi and six other government officials to death for "high treason."

May 19: Yemen's Houthi movement **says** it fired a ballistic missile towards Saudi Arabia's capital Riyadh. The Saudi-led coalition says it intercepted the missile 200 km west of the city.

May 30: Oman **mediates** between the Saudi-backed Hadi government and the Houthi rebels over a U.N. plan for peace talks.

June 5: The Houthis **ban** U.N. Special Envoy for Yemen Ismail Ould Cheikh Ahmed for abandoning his neutrality and not respecting U.N. resolutions, according to Houthi spokesman Mohammed Abdul-Salam.

June 15: Houthi rebels **fire** a missile at a United Arab Emirates ship carrying medical supplies in the Red Sea. One person is injured in the attack.

The U.N. **urges** warring parties in Yemen to agree to a U.N.-negotiated deal over the management of port city Hodeidah and resuming government salary payments.

June 17: The Saudi-backed Yemen government **agrees** to the U.N. two-point solution regarding the Hodeidah port.

July 22: The Houthis **fire** a Burkan-2 ballistic missile at an oil refinery in Saudi Arabia.

July 26: Houthi rebels **launch** a Scud missile, targeting at an oil facility near the port city of Yanbu in Saudi Arabia.

July 29: The Houthis **claim** an attack on a United Arab Emirates ship off the western coast of Yemen. No casualties or damage are reported.

Aug. 23: Houthi fighters **call** their main ally, ex-president Ali Abdullah Saleh, "evil" and condemn his description of them as a "militia." The statements highlight a growing rift between Saleh and the Houthis.

Aug. 24: Ex-president Ali Abdullah Saleh **holds** a mass rally in Sanaa to celebrate 35 years since the founding of the General People's Congress (GPC) party.

Aug. 27: Yemeni colonel and close adviser to Saleh is **killed** in clashes with Houthi rebels at a check-point in the southern neighborhood of Hadda.

Aug. 31: Former president Saleh **demands** the arrest of the Houthi gunmen who killed his close adviser.

Early Sept.: Leaders from Saleh's GPC party and the Houthis **meet** to fix the rift between both groups.

Sept. 24: President Hadi says that a military solution is more likely to solve Yemen's crisis. "The military solution is the more likely one for the Yemen crisis in light of the intransigence of the Houthi and Saleh coup militias which continue to take orders from Iran," Hadi **says** in an interview on the sidelines of the U.N. General Assembly.

Sept. 25: Yemen's Houthi forces **detain** a U.S. citizen in Sanaa.

Oct. 1: The Houthis **say** they shot down a U.S. surveillance drone in the capital of Sanaa.

Oct. 29: Saudi Arabian Foreign Minister Adel al Jubeir **says** Iran is blocking peace efforts in Yemen and is still smuggling weapons to the Houthis.

Nov. 4: Saudi Arabia **says** it intercepted a ballistic missile that was fired from Yemen near King Khaled Airport in Riyadh.

Nov. 6: Saudi Arabia **blames** Iran for the Houthi missile attack on Riyadh airport.

Nov. 7: Saudi Arabian Foreign Minister Adel al Jubeir **charges** Iran with an act of war following the Houthi missile attack on Riyadh.

The Saudi-led coalition **closes** all air, land and sea ports to the Arabian Peninsula in order to stem the flow of supplies and arms to the Houthis from Iran.

Nov. 8: Iranian President Hassan Rouhani **says** the Houthi missile attack on Saudi Arabia was a reaction to Saudi aggression. "How should the Yemeni people react to bombardment of their country. So they are not allowed to use their own weapons? You stop the bombardment first and see if the Yemenis would not do the same," Rouhani says.

The White House **condemns** the Houthi missile attack on Saudi Arabia that occurred on November 4.

Nov. 12: The Houthis **threaten** to attack warships and oil tankers in retaliation for Saudi Arabia closing Yemen's ports.

Nov. 22: The Saudi-led coalition **says** it going to reopen Yemen's Hodeida port to allow humanitarian aid through to the capital of Sanaa.

Nov. 24: Remannts of four ballistic missiles fired into Saudi Arabia by the Houthis appear to have been designed and manufactured in Iran, a confidential U.N. report **says**.

Dec. 2: Ali Abdullah Saleh publicly **splits** from his alliance with the Houthis. He calls for a "new page" in his relationship with the Saudi-led coalition.

Dec. 4: Ex-president Saleh is **killed** by the Houthis in a roadside ambush near Sanaa.

Dec. 19: Saudi Arabia **intercepts** a ballistic missile over southern Riyadh. The Houthis claim responsibility for the attack, which was targeting the royal Yamama Palace in the capital. No damage is reported.

2018

Jan. 9: Houthi rebels **threatened** to block the Red Sea shipping lane if the Saudi-led coalition keeps moving towards the Hodeidah port. "If the aggressors keep pushing toward Hodeidah and if the political solution hits wall, there are some strategic choices that will be taken as a no return point, including blocking the international navigation in the Red Sea," Houthis' Ansarullah political council chief, Saleh al-Samad, said.

Jan. 10: The Saudi-led coalition **said** it foiled an attack on a Saudi oil tanker by Houthi fighters near the Hodeidah port. The coalition destroyed a boat carrying explosives headed towards the tanker, coalition spokesman Colonel Turki al-Maliki said.

Jan. 11: The Houthis **fired** a ballistic missile at a special forces camp and a facility for helicopter gunships in the Saudi border province of Najran. Saudi air defence forces shot down the missile mid-air without any casualties, Colonel Turki al-Malki, spokesman for the Saudi-led coalition, **said**.

Jan. 12: A UN panel **concluded** that Iran violated an arms embargo imposed on Yemen by failing to prevent the Houthi rebels from obtaining Iranian missiles. The report did not say Iran had supplied missiles to the Houthi rebels, but said the Islamic Republic was in "noncompliance" with Resolution 2216, for failing to keep such weapons out of Yemen.

Jan. 16: Houthi rebels **said** they fired a short-range ballistic missile toward a regional airport in the Saudi border province of Jazan. Saudi defense forces **said** they shot down the missile over Jazan. "This hostile action by the Houthi group, which is backed by Iran, proves the Iranian regime's continuous support for the armed Houthi group by providing them with capabilities, which is in violation of UN resolutions," said spokesman for the Saudi-led coalition, Colonel Turki al-Malki.

Jan. 18: The Houthis **fired** a missile into the border province of Najran in Saudi Arabia. The missile targeted an air defense operations center and inflicted heavy damage to an air defense base in the Khadhra crossing point in Najran.

Jan. 25: Danny Lavon Burch, a U.S. citizen held captive by Houthi rebels since September 2017, was **released** and taken to Oman. He was accompanied to Oman by Mohammed Abdel-Salam, a senior Houthi leader.

Jan. 30: Houthi rebels **said** they fired a long-range ballistic missile at King Khaled International Airport in Riyadh. This is the second time the Houthis targeted the Saudi airport.

Feb. 10: Houthi spokesman Mohammad Abdul Salam **met** with Iranian Foreign Minister Javad Zarif in Tehran. Zarif **outlined** Iran's four-point peace plan for Yemen and stressed the need for an immediate stop to the war. He also called for the immediate shipment of humanitarian aid to Yemeni civilians.

The Arab coalition's Patriot air defense systems **intercepted** a ballistic missile fired by the Houthis from the Ras Kutayb area in the Hodeidah province. The missile was destroyed before reaching its intended target, suspected to be al-Mukha city in the western Yemeni province of Taiz.

Feb. 12: Major General Gameel al-Mamari, a high-ranking Houthi official, **defected** to the Yemeni army. Al-Mamari was a spokesman for the Houthis' air defence forces and a deputy director of the military forum, a group of high-ranking army officers in Sanaa.

Feb. 13: The Houthis **agreed** to join a new round of peace talks with the General People's Congress party in Oman. The peace talks will take place as soon as a new UN Peace Envoy to Yemen is announced.

Senior Houthi field commander Abu Taha al-Ghalisi was **killed** in shelling on Houthi positions in the southwestern city of Taiz. Al-Ghalisi was responsible for leading Houthi fronts north of Taiz.

Feb. 14: The Saudi military **repelled** a cross border attack by Houthi rebels in the southern border town of Nathran. Around 25 Houthi militants were killed and other wounded. Saudi helicopters also destroyed three Houthi military vehicles. This was the second cross border attack by the Houthis in less than a week.

Feb. 16-26: The United States, Britain and France **drafted** a UN Security Council resolution that condemned Iran for failing to stop its ballistic missiles from falling into the hands of the Houthis. The draft also called for renewed UN sanctions on Yemen and would allow the UN Security Council to impose targeted sanctions for "any activity related to the use of ballistic missiles in Yemen." Russia **vetoed** the resolution. The UN Securty Council subsequently passed a Russian-drafted resolution that renewed the embargo and panel's mandate but left out the Iran-Houthi issue.

Feb. 21: Mohammed Ali al Houthi **submitted** a letter to the United Nations to end the three-and-a-half-year war. The document titled "An Initiative to End the Tragedies Caused by the Aggression on Yemen" criticized the U.N. Security Council for failing "to prevent the interference and aggression against Yemen as well as the massacres committed daily against the Yemeni citizens." The letter also included points for ending the conflict, such as forming a reconciliation comittee, presidential and parliamentary elections, international guarantees to begin reconsturction and compensation for damages, and preventing any aggression from foreign countries against Yemen.

Feb. 27: The Houthis **refused** to sign a peace agreement that was built on discussions between the internationally recognized government and themselves, according to outgoing UN envoy to Yemen Ismail Ould Cheikh Ahmed. The Houthis rejected security arrangements that required them to pull out of cities and hand over weapons to a neutral military committee. "It became clear that the Al Houthis were not prepared to make concessions on the proposed security arrangements. This has been a major stumbling block towards reaching a negotiated solution," Ahmed said in his last briefing to the U.N. Security Council.

March 1: Coalition airstrikes **killed** more than 100 Houthi rebels and injured dozens of fighters in the western Hodeidah district.

March 21: Houthi rebels violenty **disbanded** a protest by dozens of supporters of ex-president Ali Abdullah Saleh in the Yemeni capital. A number of protestors were detained and some injures were reported.

March 25: The Houthis **fired** seven missiles at four Saudi cities - three at the capital Riyadh, one at the southwest city of Khamis Mushait, one at southern Najran and two at Jizan. The Houthi Ministry of Defense claimed the missiles hit seven different targets inside Saudi Arabia, including four airports. But the Saudi coalition denied the claims, saying all missiles were intercepted and destroyed. Fragments from the intercepted missiles killed an Egyptian resident. It is the first death on Saudi soil since the military intervention began.

March 29: Houthi rebels **fired** a ballistic missile from the northern Yemeni province of Saada at the Saudi city of Jazan. Saudi air defences intercepted the missile before it could strike its target.

March 30: The Yemeni army **destroyed** a Houthi weapons stockpile in Saada province. The strike coincided with a coalition raid on Houthi militias in the northern province. Houthi militants launched a ballistic missile at Saudi Arabia from the province the night before.

March 31: Saudi air defense forces **intercepted** a missile fired by the Yemeni Houthis. The missile targeted a Saudi National Guard base in the southern city Najran, a rebel-run news agency reported. An Indian resident was injured by falling debris in the attack.

April 2: Saleh al Samad, the head of the Houthi Political Council in Sanaa, **said** the rebels were "ready to buy weapons from any country that wants to sell to us, be it Russia or Iran." But he demanded the weapons be delivered to Sanaa to bypass the coalition blockade. Samad made the comments during a graduation ceremony speech for Houthi military cadets in Sanaa.

April 3: Houthi rebels **struck** a Saudi Arabian oil tanker with a missile west of Hodeidah in international waters. A coalition warship **intervened** and escorted the tanker, which sustained minimal damage, northwards. The Houthis said the attack was in response to a coalition airstrike on the rebel-held Hodeidah port that killed 14 people, including women and children, the day before.

April 4: Saudi Arabia **intercepted** a Houthi missile that was intended for southern Jizan.

April 6: The Houthis **fired** a missile at the southern city Najran, Saudi Arabia. Saudi defense forces intercepted the missile. No damage or casualties were reported.

April 11: The Houthis **launched** a Burkan 2-H ballistic missile at the Saudi capital Riyadh and also targeted oil facilities in southern Najran and Jizan, according to the rebel's Al Masirah television network. The missile traveled more than around 500 miles into Saudi Arabia before it was intercepted by Saudi air defenses. The Saudi-led coalition said it had also shot down two drones in southern Saudi Arabia. The Houthis claimed they targeted some areas with Qasif-1 drones.

April 12: Saudi air defense forces **intercepted** a Houthi missile targeting southern Jizan.

April 13: "As long as the aggression continues, our military capabilities will grow and develop," **said** Abdul Malik al-Houthi, the leader of the rebel group. The Houthis also **fired** a missile at Saudi Arabia for a third day in a row. The missile targeted southern Jizan but was intercepted by Saudi defense systems.

April 15: Iran supplied the Houthis with drones used to attack Saudi Arabia, the Yemeni government **alleged**. The drones were "made in Iran" and it was "impossible to manufacture them locally," said Yemen's internationally recongized government.

April 19: The Houthis shot down a U.S.-drone over Hodeidah, according to **Middle East Monitor**.

Saleh al Sammad, the head of the Houthis' Supreme Political Council, was **killed** in Saudi airstrikes on Hodeidah province, Al Masirah TV reported. Mahdi al Mashat was elected as Sammad's successor. "This crime will not break the will of our people and state ... [and] will not pass without accountability," Abdul Malik al Houthi said. "The forces of this aggression led by Washington and the Saudi regime are legally responsible for such a crime and all its implications."

April 22: The Houthis **fired** a ballistic missile at southern Najran. Saudi air defences intercepted the missile, "but the shrapnel scattered over residential areas and cause a fire at a farm belonging to a citizen, without causing any injuries," the Saudi Press Agency said.

April 23: Saudi Arabia **intercepted** two ballistic missiles at Saudi Aramco oil production facility in southern Jizan. The Houthis claimed responsibility on its Al Masirah TV.

April 24: Iranian Foreign Minister Javad Zarif **accused** the U.S. of fabricating evidence that Houthi missiles launched against Saudi Arabia were manufactured in Iran.

April 26: Saudi Arabia **intercepted** four ballistic missiles from Houthi rebels over southwestern Jizan. Falling debris from the interception killed one person.

April 29: The Houthis **vowed** to intensify rocket atacks on Saudi Arabia and said they are manufacturing their own ballistic missiles.

Three Saudi soldiers **died** in clashes with the Houthis along the Yemen-Saudi Arabia border, the Saudi Press Agency said.

May 3: The UN's Yemen envoy Martin Griffiths **arrived** in Omani to meet with Houthi officials to try and revive peace talks.

May 6: Houthi rebels **launched** two ballistic missils at the southern city of Najran. Saudi air defence forces intercepted the missiles. Debris from the missiles fell on residential neighborhoods but no injuries or damage were reported. "This hostile action by the Houthi militias proves the continued involvement of the Iranian regime," said Saudi coalition spokesman Col. Turki al Maliki.

May 9: The Houthis **fired** missiles at economic targets in Riyadh. Saudi Arabia intercepted one missile and another landed in an uninhabited area in the desert south of the capital. Col. Turki al Maliki said the Houthis also "failed to launch a short-range Badr-type rocket" toward Najran but it also landed in an desert area.

May 11: Some 40 Houthis were **killed** during clashes with Yemeni forces outside the city of Hodeidah.

May 14: Houhi rebels **launched** a ballistic missile at Saudi Aramco in southern Jizan province. The missile landed in the open desert and no damage was inflicted, the Saudi-led coalition said.

May 19: Saudi Arabia **intercepted** ballistic missiles from the Houthis, which were targeting the city of Khamis Mushait.

May 22: The U.S. **sanctioned** five Iranians it said provided Yemen's Houthis with technical expertise and waeponry to launch attacks against Saudi Arabia.

May 29: Yemeni forces **advanced** within 20 kilometers of the Houthi-held Hodeidah port.[723]

In this sense l believe that future of yemen belongs to mostly on the base How houthis take a step in resolving the conflict without Yemen's rebels to have a role in their country's future, would not certainly be possible unless they take some steps towards conflictresolution voicing optimism that a recent peace deal between the government and southern separatists could lead to a wider political solution to years of war.
Today key member in the Saudi-led coalition backing Yemen's government against the Houthi rebels – has been urging all sides to maintain momentum for a political resolution.

"Such an agreement must take account of the legitimate aspirations of all parts of Yemeni societyin which it should include the Houthis,"

Although "Houthi militias have wreaked havoc on the country, but they are a part of Yemeni society and they will have a role in its future." a power-sharing deal between the government and the secessionist Southern Transitional Council, signed in Riyadh could certainly pave the way for a wider peace deal.

"The agreement solidifies the anti-Houthi coalition and provides a more robust basis for reaching a political solution, "as a result, The so-called Riyadh agreement would see Yemen's government return to Aden however to get a concrete diplomatic

---

723 *Cameron Glenn was a senior program assistant at the U.S. Institute of Peace and the primary author of this article. Mattisan Rowan, a program assistant at the U.S. Institute of Peace, updated this report.*

solution, When it comes to dealing with Iran, they should not fall for the false choice between war on the one hand or a flawed [nuclear deal] on the other," because "This moment requires a renewed, robust and realistic diplomatic effort to reach a more sustainable agreement," so l still strongly believe that there is room for collective diplomacy to succeed, Because the region needs now a stronger and A "meaningful political process" rather than having conflicts with each others so **Yemeni peace** process need to refer to **the** proposals and negotiations to pacify **the Yemeni** Crisis by arranging **a** power transfer scheme within **the** country and later cease-fire attempts within **the** raging civil war.

Printed in Great Britain
by Amazon

48158485R00089